Libraries in Africa

Pioneers, Policies, Problems

by
Anthony Olden

The Scarecrow Press, Inc.
Lanham, Md., and London

SCARECROW PRESS, INC.

Published in the United States of America
by Scarecrow Press, Inc.
4720 Boston Way
Lanham, Maryland 20706

4 Pleydell Gardens, Folkestone
Kent CT20 2DN, England

Copyright © 1995 by Anthony Olden.

British Cataloguing-in-Publication Information Available

Library of Congress Cataloging-in-Publication Data

Olden, Anthony.
Libraries in Africa : pioneers, polices, problems / by Anthony Olden.
p.   cm.
Includes bibliographical references and index.
1. Libraries—Africa, Sub-Saharan—History. 2. Libraries—Nigeria—History.
Z857.A1048   1995   027.067—dc20   95-40557   CIP

ISBN 0-8108-3093-0 (cloth : alk. paper)

♾™ The paper used in this publication meets the minimum requirements of American National Standard for Information Sciences—Permanence of Paper for Printed Library Materials, ANSI Z39.48–1984.
Manufactured in the United States of America.

For Ronald Benge

Contents

Maps

Photographs

1. Three library pioneers in Africa: B. Barton-Eckett (courtesy of Arts, Libraries and Museums Department, Durham); Edith Jessie Carnell (photograph by Walter Webber, Morecambe, courtesy of Mary Piggott); and Ethel S. Fegan (courtesy of the Mistress and Fellows of Girton College, Cambridge).
2. Ethel S. Fegan and the members of the Benin Library Committee, 1941 (Mistress and Fellows of Girton College).
3. Sir Alan Burns, governor of the Gold Coast, at the Kumasi Durbar, 12 December 1946 (photograph by the West African Photographic Service, Regional Information Office, Gold Coast, courtesy of the Royal Commonwealth Society Collections, Cambridge University Library).
4. Early days of the Gold Coast Library Board's mobile service (West African Photographic Service, courtesy of Evelyn J.A. Evans).
5. The Zanzibar book exhibition, 1955: Charles Richards, the sultan of Zanzibar, and the British resident, Sir Henry Potter (photograph by Capital Arts Studio, Zanzibar, courtesy of C.G. Richards and the School of Oriental and African Studies [SOAS], London).
6. Sir Evelyn Baring, governor of Kenya, and Charles Richards at an East African Literature Bureau display, Nairobi (photograph by Department of Information, Nairobi, Kenya, C.G. Richards and SOAS).
7. The West African Library Association conference, Ibadan, 1956 (Evelyn J.A. Evans).
8. The opening of the Padmore Research Library, Accra, 30 June 1961: Kwame Nkrumah, president of Ghana, and Evelyn Evans (Evelyn J.A. Evans).

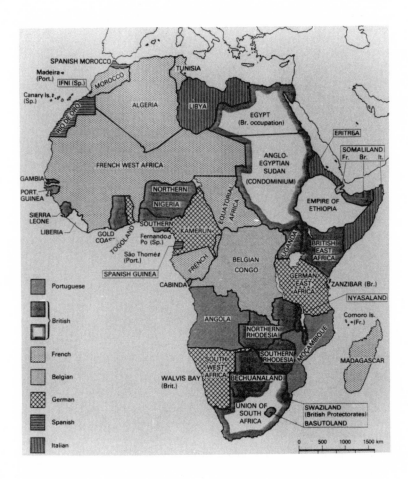

Political outline of Africa under colonial rule, 1914 (reprinted, with permission, from *Africa South of the Sahara* [London: Europa, 1992]).

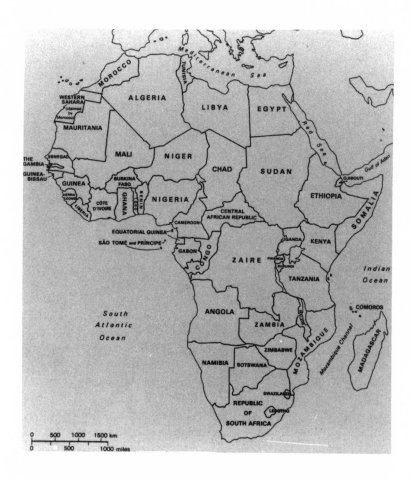

Political outline of contemporary Africa (reprinted, with permission, from *Africa South of the Sahara* [London: Europa, 1992]).

Introduction

Early in 1993 *The Lancet* published an appeal for doctors to donate their previous year's issues of the journal to a library in Africa and to commit themselves to continuing to supply such "delayed subscriptions" on an annual basis. Back sets of major medical journals were not a problem, the letter stated, but current material was: "For many African librarians it is not merely a matter of dividing a budget—there simply is no money left." The letter came from Book Aid International (BAI, at the time entitled the Ranfurly Library Service), the British charity that had set up the International Campus Book Link program to supply material to a number of research libraries in Africa.[1] Other correspondence in *The Lancet* in previous months had outlined similar work by individuals, by the Australian Centre for Publications Acquired for Development, and by the World Health Organization.[2] The American Association for the Advancement of Science (AAAS), in association with U.S. scientific and learned society publishers, is supplying almost two hundred separate journal titles to research libraries in thirty-eight Sub-Saharan African countries, more than three thousand subscriptions in all.[3] Improving access for African researchers to scientific and technical information has been an activity of the AAAS Sub-Saharan Africa Program since its inauguration in 1987.

The book famine, as it has come to be called, is particularly painful for those special libraries that were amongst the first to be established under colonial rule and for the libraries in the

---

[1] Ard Jongsma, "Journals for Developing Countries" [letter], *The Lancet* 341 (1993): 376.

[2] "Journals for Developing Countries" [letters], *The Lancet* 340 (1992): 796, 1164-65; "International Library Exchange System" [letter], 1475-76.

[3] *AAAS Sub-Saharan Africa Program* (Washington, D.C.: AAAS, [1994]), 2.

universities (university colleges initially) that strove for such high standards in the 1950s and 1960s. An AAAS survey concluded that the condition of African research libraries was "indeed parlous, [although] not unalterably bleak."[4] A British librarian visiting the University of Ibadan Library reported that "lack of funding has reduced this treasure house to a sorry shadow."[5] The University of Zimbabwe Library had no foreign currency allocated to it for the purchase of books in 1991, though the Ford Foundation helped with journal subscriptions.[6] Agricultural libraries in Ghana date from 1890, when the first was established by the Ministry of Agriculture. Now they are "under-funded, under-resourced, [and] under-equipped," while the university libraries are "sorely depleted . . . to the extent that the viability of offering postgraduate courses in agriculture is seriously in doubt."[7] The Judicial Library, Freetown, Sierra Leone, has not been able to place overseas orders for law books for a number of years, and "the likelihood of this situation improving is still remote."[8] In Uganda, according to one of the staff at the Ministry of Agriculture, "the need for up-to-date literature is chronic; we expect our research officers to solve development problems of the 1990s with knowledge thirty years old. They end up trying to reinvent the wheel or are unable to carry out experiments of the 1960s with equipment of the 1990s."[9]

One of the new states created by the Nigerian government in 1991 reported that it had "almost next to nothing to show for a

[4] Lisbeth A. Levey, *A Profile of Research Libraries in Sub-Saharan Africa: Acquisitions, Outreach, and Infrastructure* (Washington, D.C.: AAAS, Sub-Saharan Africa Program, 1993), 21.

[5] Martyn Thomas, "The Sharp Contrast between Resources of Rich and Poor" [letter], *Library Association Record* 94 (1992): 504.

[6] *Annual Report of the Librarian 1991* (Harare: University of Zimbabwe Library, no date), 4-5.

[7] Council for Scientific and Industrial Research and the International Service for National Agricultural Research [of the Netherlands], *Review of the Ghana Agricultural Research System*, vol. 1, *Report* (The Hague: International Service for National Agricultural Research [ISNAR], 1991), 41.

[8] . . . , Office of the Master and Registrar, High Court, Freetown, to BAI, 6 September 1991, Sierra Leone—Special Requests file, BAI, London. People's names and in some instances the names of their organizations are omitted from references to BAI files for reasons of confidentiality.

[9] . . . , Farming Systems Programme, Ministry of Agriculture, Entebbe, to BAI, no date [1992], Uganda—General file, BAI.

State library," while the two third-level education institutions (a college of education and a polytechnic) that had just been established were in dire need of textbooks and reference material.[10] Muhimbili Medical Centre, Tanzania, has not been able to buy textbooks for "a long time" because of financial constraints.[11] A British surgeon working in Uganda explains that none of the upcountry hospitals have functioning libraries: "We met one doctor who said, 'I come here with my head. If it is in my head, we can do it; if not, we can't.' This is an especially sad state of affairs as so much has been written especially for African upcountry hospitals, and not only is this material not present in these hospital libraries, but it is not even available in the country at large."[12]

A Canadian publishing consultant reported in 1993 that "Zambia is not simply hungry for books; it is starved for them."[13] On a visit to Ethiopia in 1992, the director of Book Aid International found that City Hall Library in Addis Ababa had had no foreign exchange with which to buy books in eighteen years, while the National Library Service was in much the same kind of situation.[14] Bulawayo Public Library, Zimbabwe, reports that "without the assistance which we receive from overseas the Library would very rapidly collapse."[15] The Malawi National Library Service was unable to place a single overseas order for a book in 1992; the "little money available" was used for the purchase of local material.[16] In Uganda the Public Libraries Board is short of stock because of the very difficult economic situation in the

---

[10] . . . , Ministry of Education, Uyo, Akwa Ibom State, to BAI, 31 January 1992, Nigeria—Completed Special Requests file, BAI.

[11] BAI evaluation form, completed by . . . Muhimbili Medical Centre, Dar es Salaam, 20 April 1993, Tanzania—Completed Special Requests file, BAI.

[12] . . . , to BAI, 16 July 1994, Thank You Letters, Requests, Proposals N-Z 1994 file, BAI.

[13] Ian Montagnes, "Children's Publishing in Zambia: Report of Findings on a Visit 13-16 April 1993," Appendix V, *The Zambia Children's Book Project* (Oxford: CODE-Europe, 1994).

[14] Sara Harrity, "Visit to Ethiopia 11th-14th May 1992," BAI.

[15] Bulawayo Public Library, *Seventh Triennial Report for the Period 1st July, 1989 to 30th June, 1992* (Bulawayo: Bulawayo Public Library, 1992), 2.

[16] . . . , National Library Service, Capital City, Lilongwe, to BAI, 15 January 1992 and 5 January 1993, Malawi—Country Information file, BAI.

country.[17]   In a building with a capacity for forty thousand
volumes Kampala Public Library has around thirteen thousand,
more than half of which are "old and obsolete. But in spite of
this and because of lack of a better alternative, the library is
well used."[18] Due to the "disastrous state" of the Sierra Leone
economy, schools in that country not only request books for their
libraries from the Sierra Leone Library Board (which requests
them from Book Aid International), but also for prizes to give to
pupils at the annual prize-giving ceremonies.[19] A Tanzanian
branch librarian reports that "for almost a decade now, the
public library network has had no foreign exchange allocation,"
and Book Aid has been the "sole assured major source" of
stock.[20] A "small public library in the Capital of the tiny
Islands of Zanzibar" told the charity that "truly speaking, we
have benefited before from your services; but this has been
mainly due to friends who visited London and collected a box or
two for us. I can assure you that we have found your books most
useful, and we thank you a lot."[21]

Disheartening though the situation is, there is constant
striving to bring about improvement through self-help and
other means. Graduates of the University of Ghana medical
school have donated enough money to pay for subscriptions to
seventeen of the journals that the medical library takes.   The
Zimbabwe Ministry of Health pays for the publication of
Current Health Information Zimbabwe, a quarterly digest of
abstracts on local health issues. This is a spin-off of *MEDLINE*
on CD-ROM, which the university medical library stocks, and
it is distributed free to health professionals throughout the
country in an attempt to compensate those in the provinces for
their lack of access to current journal literature.[22]

---

17 BAI project proposal form, completed by . . . , Public Libraries Board, Kampala,
to BAI, 23 February 1993, Uganda—Completed Special Requests file, BAI.

18 . . . , Kampala Public Library, to BAI, 28 June 1994, Thank You Letters,
Requests, Proposals N-Z 1994 file, BAI.

19 . . . , Sierra Leone Library Board, Freetown, 4 September 1991, to BAI, Sierra
Leone—General file, BAI.

20 . . . , Tanzania Library Service, Tabora, 14 October 1991, to BAI, Tanzania—
Completed Special Requests file, BAI.

21 . . . , Zanzibar Public Library, Ministry of Education, Zanzibar Revolutionary
Government, 4 November 1991, to BAI, Tanzania—General file, BAI.

22 Levey, *Profile of Research Libraries*, 6, 16.

The residents of one Ugandan village founded a center for children orphaned by the war and by AIDS. It is staffed by Ugandan teachers who volunteer their time but need books, magazines and health care information.[23] A library opened in Gwanda, the capital of Matabeleland South, Zimbabwe, in 1992. It was established by the Edward Ndlovu Memorial Trust, named after the late member of parliament and supported by money raised locally and overseas. "Since there is no public library of any significance in the province," the Trust reported, "we hope this one will help to raise the level of intellectual life . . . and make it unnecessary for people to travel to Bulawayo for books." Six months after the opening the Trust found it "most encouraging . . . to see the library packed full during school holidays, with children of all ages developing a habit of reading for pleasure."[24] For those who borrowed books there was a small annual subscription charge, but non-subscribers were permitted to read in the library, and in 1994 many unemployed local people undertaking private study were doing so.[25] The fortunes of the Zambia Library Service altered for the better in 1992 following a change of government. For many years the service "had depended upon donations for its continued existence."[26] Now the book fund had been increased from fifty thousand to ten million kwacha, and money was made available for the purchase of six reconditioned vehicles for service to the rural areas. A brighter era seemed in prospect.

Past and Present

Most of the issues relating to information and libraries in contemporary Africa go back further than is realized. A 1944 Colonial Office report referred to "the dearth of reading material . . . characteristic of most colonial areas . . . . These famine conditions affect the schools, the young adolescents who

---

[23] . . . , to BAI, 13 January 1993, Uganda—General file, BAI.

[24] "Edward Ndlovu Memorial Library: Progress Report," [1993]; . . . Edward Ndlovu Memorial Trust, to BAI, 24 March 1991 and 26 February 1993, Zimbabwe—Completed Special Requests A numbers file, BAI.

[25] "Edward Ndlovu Memorial Library: Progress Report, May 1994," Thank You Letters, Requests, Proposals N-Z 1994 file, BAI.

[26] Zambia Library Service, *Annual Report 1992* (Lusaka: Zambia Library Service, 1993).

have just finished school, and the literate adults."[27] "Today there is a great need for books [in the Gambia]," Ethel S. Fegan reported in 1942, "and they are hard to come by . . . . There is a large number of people ready and eager to avail themselves of any opportunity for reading."[28] To W.M. Macmillan in wartime West Africa it was clear that "for reasons beyond all control, the book shortage is the dominating fact."[29] R.A. Flood said in 1951 that "lack of Government enthusiasm" appeared to have been the delaying factor in establishing public libraries in Sierra Leone and the Gambia.[30]

A Zimbabwean publisher planning a mobile bookshop in 1992 got the idea from India, yet the Christian Council of Kenya operated such a service thirty years earlier.[31] A conference on textbook provision and library development in Africa took place in Manchester in 1991. It was attended by ministers of education from many countries, by representatives of donor agencies and others. Summing up the proceedings the U.K. Overseas Development Administration (ODA) spokesman said that "the obvious and immediate needs are to develop the skills of indigenous writers, build vibrant local publishing industries, and allocate more funds overall to providing textbooks and library books."[32] Yet this is what the East African Literature Bureau was attempting to do from its inception in 1948. Speaking at a UNESCO seminar in 1953 its director, Charles Richards, said its fields of activity included: "(a) textbooks for schools; (b) general literature and the tutoring of African authors; (c) the publication of a magazine; (d) the development of libraries; (e) the establishment of a

---

27 Colonial Office, Advisory Committee on Education in the Colonies, *Mass Education in African Society* (London: His Majesty's Stationery Office, 1944), par. 68.

28 Ethel S. Fegan, "Report on Library Needs in British West Africa," 1942, p.9, West Africa—Library Development 1936-1945 file, Carnegie Corporation of New York (CCNY) archives.

29 W.M. Macmillan to Sir Angus Gillan, 7 December 1944, BW8/2, Public Record Office (PRO), London.

30R.A. Flood, *Public Libraries in the Colonies* (London: Library Association,1951), 31.

31 . . . , to BAI, 4 March 1992, Zimbabwe General file, BAI; photograph, PP.MS. 12/64, C.G. Richards papers, School of Oriental and African Studies (SOAS), London.

32 *Proceedings of the Conference on Textbook Provision and Library Development in Africa, Manchester, October 1991* (Manchester: British Council, 1992), 24.

business section with a publishing fund to develop the sale of the bureau's publications and assist in the general development of bookselling."[33] The Bureau's limitations as a library service were due to the financial curbs placed by the authorities. Today's curbs are no longer placed by colonial but by independent governments. In a number of instances present government support amounts to little more than paying the salaries of those who staff libraries that have often been built by foreign donors and sometimes stocked by them as well. Times are indeed hard, but more evidence that some information is considered vital enough to be worth paying for would be welcome.

Scope and Limitations

The core of this book is a series of case studies of services that were established from the 1930s to the 1960s. They were set up with the stated intention of serving the public as a whole or a particular section of the public. But because the educational function of the "public" library in Africa is paramount anyway, and because a wider picture is more illuminating, contrasts and comparisons are made with academic and other libraries. The case studies are set in the context of their times but also looked at from the perspective of present-day issues and problems. An account is given of what led up to the introduction of each service, of the policies followed and the reasons behind them, and of the noteworthy events of the first few years. Attention is paid to the people who introduced the services, the intention being to "leave the dead some room to dance," as Wole Soyinka put it.[34] Happily quite a number are still with us, and there is an actual dance—a British Council Slow Foxtrot—among the footnotes in chapter 5. The dancers, of course, are the ones who left the records—the records that have survived and been known to and accessible to this author—and therefore, the picture is necessarily partial. The recollections of African library users and staff, if recorded, would be of great value. And the nonusers? Some of those excluded because of the color of

---

[33] C.G. Richards, "The Work of a Literature Bureau," in *Development of Public Libraries in Africa: The Ibadan Seminar* (Paris: UNESCO, 1954), 88.

[34] I am indebted to John McCracken, "African History in British Universities," *African Affairs* 92 (1993): 239-53 for bringing this to my attention.

their skin or because they could not afford the subscription fee would certainly have much to say, but for the nonliterate rural masses the library services discussed here would be beyond their range of experience. As J.J. Uta, writing about the communication of health information to rural dwellers in Malawi in the 1990s, puts it: To ask someone whether he would use an information service if it were available is unrealistic, because such services do not exist.[35]

Geographic coverage is also partial: half a chapter on the Gold Coast (now Ghana), most of the rest of the book on Nigeria and Kenya. This is not to imply that these countries are typical, or that one can generalize from them, but simply to acknowledge the bounds of personal experience, access to available source material, and time. Examples from other countries are given, though almost all are from those parts of the continent that were once under British rule and followed the Anglo-American library model and its adaptations in Africa. This is a limitation, even though the Francophone countries, for example, would not be able to supply many public library examples. Commenting on continuity in developments in Senegal, Mary Niles Maack wrote in 1981 that "few Senegalese had had experience with good public library service, since there was none in French West Africa before independence."[36] Surveying the continent in 1994 the International Federation of Library Associations and Institutions' regional chairperson for Africa, Kay Raseroka, said that five Francophone countries relied entirely on the cultural centers of foreign embassies to provide reading materials to the public.[37] One Anglo-American library follower that is only touched upon in passing in this book requires detailed investigation, South Africa.

The book is a rewritten and updated version of the author's 1987 University of Illinois Ph.D dissertation. Chapter 6, "Reading Matter and Libraries for East Africans," is new, as is the the use made of the records of Book Aid International and

[35] Joseph Jabulani Uta, "Health Communication to Rural Populations in Developing Countries; With Special Reference to Malawi," Ph.D thesis, Loughborough University, 1993, 19.

[36] Mary Niles Maack, *Libraries in Senegal: Continuity and Change in an Emerging Nation* (Chicago: American Library Association, 1981), 224.

[37] H.K. Raseroka, "Changes in Public Libraries During the Last Twenty Years: An African Perspective," *Libri* 44 (1994): 155.

the inclusion of photographs. The British Library Newspaper Library, the archives of Girton College, Cambridge, and other sources have also been consulted for the first time, and a number of people have been interviewed. The underlying question has moved on somewhat from the one in the dissertation: from who benefited from libraries in Africa to why so many African libraries are now in such a weak state. Short visits to Kenya in 1989, 1991, and 1992, and to Nigeria and Tanzania in 1992, were for purposes other than research but did help provide an up-to-date picture. Short visits to China in 1989 and 1991, and to Cuba in 1994, provided the contrasts of very different developing societies.

A slightly different version of Chapter 4, "The Lagos Library," first appeared in *Libraries and Culture (The Journal of Library History)*.

Sources

The main sources drawn upon are the archival records of the providers of foreign aid: the Carnegie Corporation of New York, the British Council, and the Ford Foundation, together with the papers of C.G. Richards, founding director of the East African Literature Bureau, on deposit at the School of Oriental and African Studies, London. Some of the British Council records have been cited before by, among others, the late S.I.A. Kotei[38] and by Douglas Coombs, who has written a valuable book on the library work of the Council.[39] Some consulted at the British Council premises by this author will have been transferred to the Public Record Office by now. Kotei and Diana Rosenberg[40] have cited relevant records in Ghana and Kenya. Other material certainly exists, for example, the papers of the late John Harris, the first professional librarian to take up a permanent post in Nigeria. These were given to the University of Otago, New Zealand, where Harris had been librarian before moving to the new University College, Ibadan, in 1948.

---

[38] Samuel Isaac Asharley Kotei, "The Social Determinants of Library Development in Ghana with Reference to the Influence of British Traditions," M.Phil thesis, University of London, 1972.

[39] Douglas Coombs, *Spreading the Word: The Library Work of the British Council* (London and New York: Mansell, 1988).

[40] Diana Bryant Rosenberg, "The Colonial State and the Development of Public Libraries in Kenya prior to 1965," Fellowship thesis, Library Association, 1984.

However, the book is published in the belief that while other sources would amplify the story, they would be unlikely to alter it significantly.

Primary sources are of value when attempting to discover what happened, or at any rate what was recorded as having happened. Secondary sources may contain inaccuracies. Both C.C. Aguolu and Mary Niles Maack, for example, have surmised that the Carnegie Corporation may not have known that its six thousand dollar grant to Lagos in 1932 was going to establish a subscription library (Chapter 4).[41, 42] This was not the case: the Corporation's records contain a letter from Alan Burns, the instigator of the grant request, that includes his reasons for wanting to charge.[43] Hugh Macmillan says that as senior representative of the British Council in West Africa from 1943 to 1945 W.M. Macmillan "supervised the inauguration of the first effective network of public libraries."[44] This is not correct. Mona Macmillan says that "Miss Ferguson went to Lagos and created a fine Nigerian National Library."[45] She did nothing of the kind (Chapter 5).

Letters contain comment that would have been unlikely to get into print. Colonel Turner of the Kenya Rural Libraries scheme wanted to get rid of his chief librarian in 1934 on the grounds that the man was being paid more than the scheme could continue to afford (Chapter 3). But he confided to the Carnegie president that not only was the man the wrong class for the colony but that he was also being "most indiscreet in his domestic arrangements," going on to give full details.[46] Turner's letter is as revealing about some members of the ruling class of

---

[41] C.C. Aguolu, "The Foundations of Modern Libraries in Nigeria," *International Library Review* 9 (1977): 479.

[42] Mary N. Maack, "The Colonial Legacy in West African Libraries: A Comparative Analysis," in *Advances in Librarianship* 12 (New York: Academic Press, 1982):196.

[43] A.C. Burns to F.P. Keppel, 7 May 1929, Nigeria (West Africa), Support of a Program of Library Development file, CCNY archives.

[44] Hugh Macmillan, introduction to *Africa and Empire: W.M. Macmillan, Historian and Social Critic,* ed. Hugh Macmillan and Shula Marks (London: Temple Smith for the Institute of Commonwealth Studies, 1989), 27.

[45] Mona Macmillan, *Champion of Africa: W.M. Macmillan, The Second Phase* (Long Wittenham, Oxfordshire: Mona Macmillan, 1985), 182.

[46] Ralph Turner to Keppel, 21 April 1934, Kenya Colony—Library Development file, CCNY archives.

colonial Kenya as any number of government blue books.

The photographs are a selection from what could be traced. Those from the collection of Evelyn J.A. Evans, founding director, Gold Coast (later Ghana) Library Board, show aspects of a new service in the final years of colonial and the first years of independent rule, even though that service is not one of the case studies in the text (it has been widely covered elsewhere). The photograph of Sir Alan Burns (Chapter 4) dates from the period of his governorship of the Gold Coast rather than that of his earlier association with the Lagos Library. Photographs of Kate Dorothy Ferguson (Chapter 5) found in her alumna file at the University of Illinois, and others traced by Marydee Ojala,[47] are unfortunately of too poor a quality to reproduce. Photographs of W.M. Macmillan and Sir Angus Gillan can be found elsewhere.[48]

Acknowledgements

I would like to repeat my thanks to Donald E. Crummey, Linda C. Smith, C.C. Stewart and, in particular, to Lawrence W.S. Auld. Sara L. Engelhardt, Patricia Haynes, and Loretta Moore assisted at the Carnegie Corporation of New York; Paul J. Kaiser, Sharon B. Laist, Ann Newhall, and Neenah Payne at the Ford Foundation; Vicki Martineau at the British Council; Rosemary Seton and Barbara Turfan at the School of Oriental and African Studies; Antje Brauer, Lesley Carver, Maggie Gardiner, Sara Harrity, Ard Jongsma and, in particular, David Membrey, at Book Aid International; and Kate Perry at Girton College, Cambridge. Terry Barringer, Royal Commonwealth Society Collections, Cambridge University Library, and the staffs of the Public Record Office and the British Library have also been helpful.

I would like to thank Evelyn Evans and Charles Richards for permission to reproduce photographs from their collections and for discussing with me their work in Ghana, Kenya, and elsewhere. D.J. Butler of the Durham Record Office checked

---

[47] "Bank of Italy Library," *Bankitaly Life*, January 1923, 5; Ethel Bogardus, "Women Take Big Roles in Bank of Italy," *San Francisco Examiner*, 22 March 1928.

[48] Macmillan is on the cover of Mona Macmillan, *Champion of Africa*. A youthful Detective-Inspector Gillan with colleagues in the Sudan Political Service in 1910 is in *Tales from the Dark Continent*, ed. Charles Allen (London: Andre Deutsch and the British Broadcasting Corporation, 1979).

the surviving records of the Durham County Library Service on my behalf, and A.L. Ward of the Arts, Libraries and Museums Department provided a copy of a photograph of B. Barton-Eckett (Chapter 3). Marydee Ojala has given me her special librarian's viewpoint on Kate Ferguson and sent me copies of documentation. Wong Heng (National Library of Singapore) searched Singaporean sources for information about her. Dorothy McCreight, Ethel Fegan's niece, wrote to say that she never heard much about the Ferguson cousin. Jennifer Fitzgerald (Queen's College, London) told me about Fegan's pioneering—and largely unrecognized—work in the field of education for librarianship while based at Cheltenham Ladies College. Mary Piggott provided the photograph of Jessie Carnell. R.G. Opondo (former librarian of the McMillan Memorial Library, Nairobi) supplied a copy of Elspeth Huxley's 1946 report, *Literature for Africans,* and other useful information.

Conversations with a number of people over the last few years about aspects of information and development have been helpful. I would like to thank Hans M. Zell and Mary Jay (the African Books Collective, Oxford); M.M. Zaki (Ahmadu Bello University, Nigeria); Sara Harrity and David Membrey (Book Aid International); John Salter (formerly British Council, Zimbabwe); Evelyn Atsodibuor (Ghana Ministry of Agriculture Library); Shiraz Durrani (London Borough of Hackney); Mary Ross-Smith (Harare City Library); Carol Priestley and Diana Rosenberg (International African Institute); Nathan Mnjama, Dennis N. Ocholla, Joseph B. Ojiambo, and the late Jonathan Kariara (Moi University, Kenya); Alli A.S. Mcharazo (Tanzania Library Service and Thames Valley University); Richard Downing, Stephen A. Roberts, J.R. Shearer and W.R. Webster (Thames Valley University); Angela and Michael Wise (Llandre, Bow Street, Dyfed); participants at the African Library Science Journals Workshop (Bayero University, Kano, Nigeria, 29-30 January 1992); participants at the Book Publishing Management Workshop (Moi University, 16-26 August 1992); and students at Thames Valley University who took my Information and the Developing World courses.

London
December 1994

Chapter 1

Library Development in Africa:
Context and Documentation

Although Europeans established a fortified trading base on the West African coast as early as 1482, most of the continent did not come under their control until the end of the nineteenth and the very beginning of the twentieth century. It was to stay under their rule for no more than sixty years, although this was far from obvious until after World War II. Sir F.D. Lugard (later Lord Lugard), who secured large parts of Africa for Britain, wrote in 1922: "We hold these countries because it is the genius of our race to colonise, to trade, and to govern."[1] Government meant the establishment of law and order to the satisfaction of the rulers, the laying down of railways and roads so as to extract minerals and crops from the interior, and the collection of taxes to pay for it all. Colonization meant permanent European settlement—or, rather, settlement that the Europeans believed would be permanent—in lands that seemed worth the taking.

British West Africa, with its reputation as the "white man's grave," was not one of these regions. Only traders, missionaries, soldiers, and administrators went there, and those who survived ultimately returned to Britain. The healthier climates and more open lands of southern and eastern Africa were more attractive. By the late nineteenth century part of what was to become the Republic of South Africa had been under European settlement for more than two hundred years. In the 1890s the whites moved north and took control of the area they were to name Rhodesia in honor of their adventurer-hero Cecil Rhodes. The possibilities for European settlement in the

---

[1] Sir F.D. Lugard, *The Dual Mandate in British Tropical Africa* (Edinburgh and London: William Blackwood and Sons, 1922), 618-19.

highlands of Kenya were seen by Lord Delamere and others; *White Man's Country* was the title given by Elspeth Huxley to her 1935 book on the making of the colony. The novelist Evelyn Waugh visited in 1931 and described it as an equatorial Barsetshire: "the Kenya settlers are not cranks of the kind who colonised New England, nor criminals and ne'er-do-wells of the kind who went to Australia, but perfectly normal, respectable Englishmen, out of sympathy with their own age." They wanted to keep going "the traditional life of the English squirearchy," a life no longer possible at home.[2]

The identification of areas where whites settled permanently is important, because it was in these areas that African educational progress was to be slowest. The settlers had more to gain from keeping Africans down. The descendants of settlers had most of all at stake. The difference between South Africa and Nigeria, two possessions whose resources made them particularly important, can be illustrated in numerous ways. The University of the Witwatersrand, whose roots go back to the beginning of the century, did not employ a black professional librarian until 1975.[3] University College, Ibadan, founded in 1948, had Nigerian librarians in the 1950s, before Nigeria had any library school. The writer Doris Lessing, who grew up in Southern Rhodesia, has pointed out what a great deal that colony had in common with South Africa, on which it patterned its laws.[4] South West Africa (now Namibia) excluded Africans from its public libraries until 1985.[5] It had been under South African control since after World War I, when Germany's colonies were taken away and parcelled out under League of Nations mandate (Tanganyika and parts of Togo and Cameroon were given to Britain). Although in Kenya the interests of the African population were declared paramount by the British colonial secretary in 1923, the Colonial Office continued to serve the whites by appointing men with South

---

[2] Evelyn Waugh, *Remote People* (London: Duckworth, 1931), 183.

[3] Reuben Musiker, *Aspects of Wits Library History* (Johannesburg: University of the Witwatersrand, The Library, 1982), 12.

[4] "Doris Lessing, Interviewed by Eve Bertelsen," *Journal of Commonwealth Literature* 21 (1986): 138-39.

[5] Andree-Jeanne Totemeyer, *Report on a Survey: The State of Public Libraries in Namibia and the Need for Training for Public/Community Libraries*, vol. 2 (Windhoek: University of Namibia, Department of Library and Information Science, 1991), 1.

African experience to key positions in agriculture, the railways, education, and local government.[6]

British West Africa was very different: no white settlers and a westernized, British-trained African elite of lawyers and others. Racial discrimination certainly existed,[7] though to a lesser extent than in Kenya, Southern Rhodesia, and South Africa. At the races in Lagos in 1931 a visitor from England was impressed to see Africans in well-cut lounge suits stopping to chat with the governor, Sir Donald Cameron, and being invited to tea in his private pavilion.[8] Cameron's deputy secretary, Alan Burns, was far too shrewd to discriminate on the basis of color. He started a monthly dining club for the leading Europeans and Africans in Lagos, as well as the Carnegie-assisted fee-charging Lagos Library. He told Colonial Office officials in 1941 that he saw no reason why a judge who happened to be African should not live in a housing area reserved by the government for senior officials just like judges who happened to be European.[9] About the same time in Kenya the Europeans who attended Sunday morning service at St. Mark's, Parklands, in Nairobi, objected to services being held for their servants in the afternoon on the grounds that they would have to sit on the same seats the following Sunday morning.[10]

The European colonizers of Africa were the Portuguese, the Dutch, the British, the French, the Belgians, the Germans, and, to a lesser extent, the Spanish and the Italians. Britain had some of the most productive and densely populated parts of the continent. Samir Amin has pointed out that British West

---

[6] Andrew Roberts, "The Imperial Mind," in the *Cambridge History of Africa*, vol. 7, *From 1905 to 1940*, ed. A.D. Roberts (Cambridge: Cambridge University Press, 1986), 46.

[7] See John Flint, "Scandal at the Bristol Hotel: Some Thoughts on Racial Discrimination in Britain and West Africa and Its Relationship to the Planning of Decolonisation, 1939-47," *Journal of Imperial and Commonwealth History* 12 (1983): 74-93.

[8] Margery Perham, *West African Passage: A Journey through Nigeria, Chad and the Cameroons, 1931-1932*, ed. A.H.M. Kirk-Greene (London and Boston: Peter Owen, 1983), 49.

[9] Cited in Flint, "Scandal," 84.

[10] Rev. W. Owen, cited in Richard Frost, *Race Against Time: Human Relations and Politics in Kenya Before Independence* (London and Nairobi: Rex Collings and Transafrica Book Distribution, 1978), 176.

Africa (Nigeria, the Gold Coast, Sierra Leone, and the Gambia), though smaller in area than French West Africa, had a larger and more concentrated population, and this made rapid exploitation much more possible. France had the Sahara, and Amin says that the conquest of Chad, for example, had more to do with romanticism than with economic interests.[11]

Sir John Macpherson, who came to Nigeria from Malaya in 1937, remembers no pressure for faster constitutional advance until World War II changed everything.[12] There had been pressure in India, of course, and in 1947 it became the first non-white part of the British Empire to achieve independence. The Sudan became independent in 1956, the Gold Coast (as Ghana) in 1957, Nigeria in 1960, Tanganyika (later Tanzania) in 1961, Uganda in 1962, Kenya in 1963, Northern Rhodesia (as Zambia) and Nyasaland (as Malawi) in 1964. The white settlers in Southern Rhodesia, who numbered about one in twenty of the population, attempted to hold onto power by declaring the colony independent in 1965. Backed by South Africa, they survived objections and sanctions from other African countries, from Britain, and from the United Nations, before finally succumbing to armed force from within. Rhodesia finally came under black majority rule as Zimbabwe in 1980. South Africa, where the whites number about one in seven today, has been self-governing since the early years of the century. Its minority rulers held onto power until 1994.

All the Belgian and almost all the French territories in Africa had been granted independence by the early 1960s. Portugal used force to hang onto its possessions until 1974.

Elites, Dependence, and Cultural Hegemony

Tea with the governor indicates that at least certain Africans had greater opportunities in some parts of Africa than in others. It can also be interpreted as collaboration with the forces of occupation, the exploiters. According to Jean-Paul Sartre the world during the colonial era was divided into men and natives with, in the middle, the go-betweens, the "hired

---

11 Samir Amin, *Neo-Colonialism in West Africa* (New York and London: Monthly Review Press, 1973), x.

12 John Macpherson, foreword to Robert Heussler, *Yesterday's Rulers: The Making of the British Colonial Service* (Syracuse, N.Y.: Syracuse University Press, 1963), xii.

kinglets, overlords, and a bourgeoisie, sham from beginning to end."[13] Sartre was writing during Algeria's war with France for independence, introducing *The Wretched of the Earth* by Frantz Fanon from Martinique in the West Indies. Fanon had worked as a psychiatrist in Algeria, until he found himself more in sympathy with the rebels than with his French employers. He eventually became the Algerian provisional government's ambassador to Ghana. But much of what he found in newly independent Africa disappointed him. The middle class—"the national bourgeoisie"—was parasitic rather than productive, and its sole concern was to get rich quick. Unlike its western counterpart, which had gone through stages of invention and exploration, the African middleclass was incapable of originality. It remembered what it had read in textbooks, but it was a caricature rather than a replica of the European middle class. It wanted the whitemen out so that it could replace them in the top positions, then assume its historic role of intermediary or gatekeeper.[14] More recently the Kenyan Ngugi wa Thiong'o has been equally scathing in his novels, criticism, and children's stories.[15]

E.A. Ayandele, the Nigerian historian, has this to say about his countrymen:[16]

> The unlettered, whose first reaction in the precolonial era was to pity the educated elite as Africans who had decivilized and devalued themselves, were eventually to turn their commiseration into consternation, as the educated elite proved themselves harbingers of British colonial rule; to sullen resignation during the colonial period; to inevitable acceptance of the leadership of this class of people in the last twenty-two years. Today the wheel has turned full circle; the unlettered are only anxious to contribute their full quota to the enlargement of the educated elite.

Ayandele maintains that the British, toward the end of the colonial period, reversed their stance and started to woo the people they had despised as caricatures up to then. They came to see that the elite was the group most likely to "retain,

---

[13] Jean-Paul Sartre, preface to Frantz Fanon, *The Wretched of the Earth* (New York: Grove Press, 1968), 7.

[14] Fanon, *Wretched of the Earth*, "The Pitfalls of National Consciousness" chapter.

[15] See, for example, Ngugi wa Thiong'o, *Njamba Nene and the Flying Bus* (Nairobi: Heinemann Kenya, 1986), and *Matigari* (Oxford: Heinemann, 1989).

[16] E.A. Ayandele, *The Educated Elite in the Nigerian Society* (Ibadan: Ibadan University Press, 1974), 2.

strengthen, and further promote the cultural, economic, and technological legacies of the colonial era and of the Western world."[17]

Fanon had said that the economic concerns were still the same as before independence: the groundnut harvest, the cocoa crop, the olive yield, or whichever produce or mineral had helped complete the economy of the colonizing country. This links up with the theory of underdevelopment that Andre Gunder Frank propounded in the 1960s. Frank wrote about Latin America, that part of the less developed world that has been longest under western influence, longest free of direct western political control, and which—with only two official languages, Spanish or Portuguese—is much less linguistically fragmented than Africa. He differentiates between undeveloped and underdeveloped: the now developed countries may once have been undeveloped, but they were never underdeveloped. The metropolitan or "home" countries of the West underdevelop their satellite colonies by sucking out their economic surplus and capital. Within a colony or ex-colony the process is repeated: the capital extracts from the provincial capitals, the provincial capitals from their provinces, and so on. The most underdeveloped areas today are the ones that had the closest ties to the metropoles in the past: the West Indies, for example, left to sink into ultra-underdevelopment once the West no longer wanted its sugar.[18]

Frank's underdevelopment and Fanon's national bourgeoisie can be taken a step further with the cultural hegemony theory of Antonio Gramsci, a founder of the Italian Communist Party and one of the most influential of twentieth-century Marxist thinkers.[19] Gramsci felt that economic and political power did not explain everything, that cultural and intellectual influence were important also. A successful ruling class is one that establishes its intellectual and moral leadership before obtaining political power. Intellectual influence on an international scale occurs also, and it is this aspect of Gramsci

---

[17] Ayandele, *Educated Elite*, 2.

[18] Andre Gunder Frank, *Latin America: Underdevelopment or Revolution. Essays on the Development of Underdevelopment and the Immediate Enemy* (New York: Monthly Review Press, 1969).

[19] The points about Gramsci are taken from James Joll, *Antonio Gramsci* (New York: Penguin, 1978).

that is particularly helpful when considering the academic and professional classes in underdeveloped countries.

The arrangements under which a number of institutions in British Africa developed into universities provide a good illustration of cultural hegemony. These included the university colleges of the Gold Coast and Ibadan (Nigeria), founded in 1948, and the University College of East Africa, Makerere (Uganda), whose roots go back to the 1920s. E.R.J. Hussey, director of education in Uganda (and later in Nigeria, where he was one of the founding members of the Lagos Library), said in 1925 that Makerere would enable Ugandans, "led by men who have not weakened through education the ties that bind them to their mother country, to progress slowly but surely towards a higher civilization and culture."[20] Lord Ashby (formerly Sir Eric Ashby), chairman of the Carnegie Corporation-funded Commission on Post-School Certificate and Higher Education in Nigeria, said that the pioneers had no choice but to accept the pattern of an English university, and that this was what Africans wanted anyway. According to Sir Alexander Carr-Saunders "it was obvious that, if Africans were to be enabled to join the ranks of the ruling classes under the colonial regime and to prepare themselves for the time—then thought to be distant—when full power would pass to them, higher education facilities in the colonies must be basically of the British pattern."[21]

The proceedings of a 1980 Rockefeller Foundation conference on strengthening the social sciences provide equally good illustrations. Kenneth Prewitt, president of the Social Science Research Council, New York, discussed the impact of U.S. social science theory and methodology and concluded that "the United States was the exporting nation or, if you prefer, the hegemonic community; and most Third World countries were the importers or, if you prefer, the dependent clients."[22] David

---

[20] Cited in Margaret Macpherson, *They Built for the Future: A Chronicle of University College 1922-1962* (Cambridge: Cambridge University Press, 1964), xii.

[21] Both cited in Bruce Pattison, *Special Relations: The University of London and New Universities Overseas, 1947-1970* (London: University of London, 1984), 161.

[22] Kenneth Prewitt, "The Impact of the Developing World on U.S. Social-Science Theory and Methodology," in *Social Sciences and Public Policy in the Developing World*, ed. Laurence D. Stifel, Ralph K. Davidson and James S. Coleman (Lexington [Massachusetts] and Toronto: Lexington Books, 1982), 5.

Court said that the early impetus for the development of social science in East Africa came from the British Ministry of Overseas Development, the Rockefeller and Ford Foundations, and the Carnegie Corporation. They believed it was important to understand the "social concomitants to economic development" and that the social sciences would contribute to this understanding.[23] They meant western-style economic development, of course, and critics such as Andre Gunder Frank argue that this is for the benefit of the West rather than of the areas in which it is taking place.

No western-trained social scientists have had more influence than the economists. Warren F. Ilchman suggested that not since the time of Aristotle and Alexander was such homage paid by former students to their teachers as by the Indonesian military to their countrymen who had taught them economics at the Army Staff and Command School in the years preceding their overthrow of the Sukarno government in 1965. After being in virtual intellectual exile under a regime that outlawed the teaching of "western economics" the U.S. trained economists found themselves government ministers. Ilchman said the tribute extends to the teachers' American teachers at Berkeley and Pittsburgh and, at a still further remove, to the teachers of these teachers at Cambridge, Massachusetts, and Cambridge, England.[24] A less indulgent interpretation of the influence of this "extraordinary team of Indonesian economists" and their associates has been given elsewhere by David Ransom.[25]

U.S. influence has predominated in the development of modern economics in Latin America, and the conservative approach of Milton Friedman and the Chicago School of Economics has had a particular impact. The support of the U.S. government and the American foundations extended from the 1950s to the mid-1970s and then stopped, because as Eduardo Venezian of the Catholic University of Chile explained: "The job of establishing economics as a respectable and useful science

[23] David Court, "The Idea of Social Science in East Africa: An Aspect of the Development of Higher Education," in Stifel and others, *Social Sciences*, 155.

[24] Warren F. Ilchman, "Hybrids in Native Soil: The Social Sciences in Southeast Asia," in Stifel and others, *Social Sciences*, 155.

[25] David Ransom, "Ford Country: Building an Elite for Indonesia," in Steve Weissman and others, *The Trojan Horse: A Radical Look at Foreign Aid* (San Francisco: Ramparts Press, 1974), 93-116.

in Latin America had been essentially accomplished."[26] After the Chilean military overthrew the Salvador Allende government in 1973, it found the services of the group that came to be known as "the Chicago boys" quite useful. According to Edgardo Boeninger, who had worked as an economist for the Eduardo Frei government of the 1960s and later served as rector of the University of Chile: "The at-the-time unchallenged hegemony of the Chicago School of Economics in the southern cone of Latin America was made possible by the fact that a phalanx of indigenous economists was trained in Chicago and became deeply committed to the theories prevalent in that particular school. Due to a complex set of political factors, the leaders of various military coups adopted that model and then proceeded to impose these policies by force."[27] This forced return to liberal economic principles caused great hardship to many in Chile. Edwin Williamson notes that in 1988 nearly half the population lived below the poverty line, while the top 5 percent received over 80 percent of the national income.[28] In the U.S. and Britain in the 1980s the gap between the better off and the poor widened as a result of the economic policies of Ronald Reagan and Margaret Thatcher. The World Bank's structural adjustment programs brought austerity to countries in Africa and elsewhere. In return for money from Washington, governments changed their policies, devalued their currencies, cut their expenditure, and told their people that there was no alternative.[29] Jean-François Bayart points out how the Bank recruits some of the ablest African intellectuals onto its staff at international-level salaries, while at the same time urging African governments to pay their own civil servants less.[30]

---

[26] Eduardo Venezian, "The Economic Sciences in Latin America," in Stifel and others, *Social Sciences*, 195.

[27] Edgardo Boeninger, "Application of the Social Sciences to Public Policies: Producers, Consumers and Mechanisms of Mediation," in Stifel and others, *Social Sciences*, 271.

[28] Edwin Williamson, *The Penguin History of Latin America* (Harmondsworth, Middlesex: Penguin, 1992), 509.

[29] See, for example, Graham Hancock, *Lords of Poverty* (London: Mandarin, 1991), chapter 4.

[30] Jean-François Bayart, *The State in Africa: The Politics of the Belly* (London and New York: Longman, 1993), xiii.

Obviously western ideas about library and information service have nothing like the impact of western economic theories on people in the developing world, but Colonel and Mrs. Turner (Chapter 3), Professor Macmillan (Chapter 5), Kate Ferguson (Chapter 5), Professor White (Chapter 8), and others have bequeathed their own small legacy of influence, and the British Public Library still lingers as a model.

Literacy, Libraries, and the 1953 UNESCO Seminar at Ibadan

According to the Nigerian historian A.E. Afigbo, literacy was the most important single innovation of foreign rule for the non-Muslim parts of Africa. It was the new magic that opened up the modern world.[31] Islam had introduced literacy to parts of the West African interior and the East African coast before the Europeans took over the continent. Ethiopia, which did not come under European domination until Mussolini's forces invaded in 1936, had had church schools and a religious language, Geez, for many centuries, but education and literacy affected only a tiny proportion of the population. As recently as 1970 over 98 percent of females aged ten years and above in rural areas were illiterate.[32] Literacy statistics can hardly be relied upon, but according to UNESCO out of 354.3 million Africans aged fifteen years and older in 1990, 177.5 million or 50 percent were illiterate.[33]

The locations of the first collection of western books in tropical Africa illustrate the connection between learning, power, and influence: schools, missions, government secretariats, law courts, and medical, veterinary, agricultural, and geological stations. The continent's southern tip, where whites had settled in the seventeenth century, had a much earlier start. It had what were known as public libraries but

---

[31] A.E. Afigbo, "The Social Repercussions of Colonial Rule: The New Social Structures," in *General History of Africa*, vol. 7, *Africa under Colonial Domination*, ed. A. Adu Boahen (Paris, London and Berkeley: UNESCO, Heinemann Educational Books and the University of California Press, 1985), 496.

[32] Central Statistics Office, Addis Ababa, cited in Margareta and Rolf Sjostrom, *How Do You Spell Development? A Study of a Literacy Campaign in Ethiopia* (Uppsala: Scandinavian Institute of African Studies, 1983), 38.

[33] *UNESCO Compendium of Statistics on Illiteracy*, 1990, cited in *Women and Literacy*, prepared by Marcela Ballara (London and Atlantic Highlands, N.J.: Zed Books, 1992), 5.

were actually fee-charging services for those whites able and willing to pay, which again illustrates the connection between books and power. In 1905 the librarian at Kimberly wrote at the request of his committee to ask his colleague at Johannesburg whether "persons of colour" were permitted to use his "free or public reading room." The question had never arisen, the reply stated, but on considering it the Johannesburg committee felt that the public interest would not be served by admitting such persons.[34] Public interest was the interest of the rulers, who happened to be white. The "native problem" was behind this according to Milton J. Ferguson, state librarian of California and one of the Carnegie Corporation of New York's consultants. Ferguson visited South Africa in 1928 and appreciated that, if libraries were supported by public funds, then the blacks might feel that they also had the right to use what was paid for out of their taxes, and this the whites would not want.[35]

Fee-charging services were started with Carnegie Corporation help in Kenya and Nigeria in the early 1930s. The British Council opened fee-charging libraries in Lagos and Accra in the 1940s and after several years handed them over to the Lagos Town Council and the specially established Gold Coast Library Board. Under Evelyn J.A. Evans, who transferred from the British Council along with her library, the Gold Coast built up a service that people spoke of as a model for the rest of Africa. Yvonne Oddon, librarian of the Musée de l'Homme, Paris, found the Gold Coast the only one of the various African territories she visited in 1952 in which public libraries had progressed beyond a very early stage of development, if indeed they existed at all. Her tour was in preparation for what was to be the fourth in a series of UNESCO-sponsored meetings on aspects of public library development. The first, on general problems, was held in Manchester, England, in 1948; the second, on the role of libraries in adult and fundamental education, in Malmö, Sweden, in 1950; the third, on Latin America, in São Paulo, Brazil, in 1951. The fourth took place at University College, Ibadan, from 27 July to 21 August 1953, with twenty-

---

[34] Cited in R.F. Kennedy, *The Heart of a City: A History of the Johannesburg Public Library* (Cape Town: Juta and Company, 1970), 500.

[35] Milton J. Ferguson, *Memorandum: Libraries in the Union of South Africa, Rhodesia, and Kenya Colony* (New York: Carnegie Corporation of New York, 1929), 30.

nine participants (eight Africans, the rest mainly Europeans working in Africa). The seminar was important, one of its earliest tangible results being the establishment of the West African Library Association. The published proceedings are valuable both as a record of the views held and of the state of libraries in the early 1950s.[36]

The assumption that the spread of public libraries would aid the spread of literacy in Africa can be traced back to this seminar. The host librarian, John Harris, and his former deputy, Jessie Carnell, happened to be interested in both public libraries and in literacy. They had written a paper earlier in which they suggested that the Western Region of Nigeria should start an experimental library service at Ibadan for three groups: those with some primary education who were literate in English, those literate only in a Nigerian language, and those at a rudimentary stage, such as the participants in a mass literacy campaign.[37]

Also significant was the fact that several participants were not librarians but others with an interest in combating illiteracy. The professor of education at the University College of the Gold Coast suggested points to bear in mind when writing material for new literates. Another speaker from the Gold Coast talked about what the mass education officer expected the public library to provide. The director of the East African Literature Bureau, Charles Richards, spoke of his work, which included bringing a variety of appropriate books and magazines into being. Barbara Mullane (who was a librarian) of the Nigerian Public Relations Department gave a paper on the place of the public library in mass education programs. She said that the library should follow up with appropriate material so that the skill learned in class would not be forgotten. One recommendation adopted at the seminar was that the UNESCO Public Library Manifesto be adopted as the basis on which national public library service be established in Africa. The manifesto states that, "as a democratic institution, operated by the people for the people, the public library should be . . . open

36 *Development of Public Libraries in Africa: The Ibadan Seminar* (Paris: UNESCO, 1954).

37 Jessie Carnell and John Harris, "Libraries in Nigeria: A Memorandum Presented to the Study Group on Education in West Africa, 1951/52," *West African Libraries* 1 (1954): 5.

for free use on equal terms to all members of the community."[38]

The appendix (pp.138-47) on the state of public library development was compiled from reports submitted by seminar participants and from other sources. It cautions that the use of the term public library in the documents from which information was drawn was somewhat elastic and could mean anything from a reading room with three to four hundred books to a library or library system with several thousand. Also, some of the libraries served Europeans but not Africans, and this was not always stated. But it would serve as a rough picture, and the statistics that follow are drawn from it.

Public libraries for Europeans existed in South Africa, the Rhodesias, Nyasaland, and Kenya. In Nigeria and the Gold Coast they were open to all races. In the Belgian Congo (later Zaire), with an estimated population of 11,259,000, there were 24 official public libraries for Europeans (132,297 books and 2,047 subscribers as of 31 December 1950) and 193 for Africans (66,651 books and 6,164 subscribers). Thus the ratio of books to subscriber was sixty-five to a European and eleven to an African, and one African out of every eighteen hundred or so people in the colony subscribed. J.M. Domont, head of the Belgian Congo's Office of Information for Natives, explained in his seminar paper: "The philosophic make-up of the Bantus is not of a positive nature; as a result there is a lack of intellectual appetite." Domont stated that the organization of libraries in the colony enabled the literate Congolese to secure books on loan wherever he might be. In his view "it would be superfluous to try to bring about any substantial changes in the present system, which is clearly equipped to cover all reading needs in the shortest possible time and at the lowest possible cost to the reader."[39]

In the Portuguese islands of São Tomé and Principe, with an estimated population of 60,500, the public library had 2,010 books, a circulation of 50 books, and 31 readers in 1949. In the Portuguese colony of Angola, with an estimated population of 4,093,000, the municipal library in Luanda had 10,116 books, 1,411 readers, and a circulation of 1,834 books in 1949. In French

---

[38] *UNESCO Bulletin for Libraries* 3 (1949): 242-44.

[39] J.M. Domont, "Reading in the Belgian Congo," in *Development of Public Libraries in Africa*, 77, 81.

Equatorial Africa, with an estimated population of 4,406,000, the governor's central library in the capital, Brazzaville, was open to the public. It had 2,500 books, mainly about the territory and about public administration. In addition more than thirty libraries (two to three hundred books each) had been organized by culture clubs in various places.

The first issue of *West African Libraries* summed up the situation: Africa was a continent "mainly devoid of public library service or even of libraries and librarianship in any real sense."[40] The British territories were the furthest advanced, except that in a majority of them the libraries or book collections (or at least the better ones) were to be used only by whites. This mirrored the situation in Europe, where public libraries were more developed in Britain than in France. In 1970 a UNESCO meeting in Kampala, Uganda, noted the almost universal lack of any form of public library service in the French-speaking countries; the participants included representatives from Senegal, the Ivory Coast, the People's Republic of the Congo, and Madagascar.[41] As for Portugal, it is unlikely that one of the less developed countries in Western Europe would have been to the fore in providing libraries for its colonies. As late as 1969 the Anglican bishop of Laurenço Marques (now Maputo), a Portuguese national, remarked to Charles Richards, then visiting Mozambique as director of the Christian Literature Fund, that as far as he could see nothing could be expected from Africans in the way of writing or contribution to thought.[42]

The Documentation

Writing at the end of the 1980s, Paul Sturges and Richard Neill dismissed much of the past literature on libraries and information in Africa as "conventional and repetitive."[43] K.J. Mchombu and K. Miti have complained about "long uncritical

---

[40] *West African Libraries* 1 (1954): 1.

[41] *Expert Meeting on National Planning of Documentation and Library Services in Africa: Kampala, Uganda, 7-15 December 1970: Final Report* (Paris: UNESCO, 1971), 3.

[42] C.G. Richards, "Mozambique, Monday 30 June 1969," in Tour Report: Africa, 22 June to 3 July 1969, PP.MS. 12/82, Richards papers.

[43] Paul Sturges and Richard Neill, *The Quiet Struggle: Libraries and Information for Africa* (London and New York: Mansell, 1990), 2.

descriptions from . . . office holders."[44] The Ford Foundation's Francis X. Sutton said that the reports and files of foundations contained "an abundance of reporting on the support that was actually given but . . . much less on the analytical or philosophical reasons for undertaking such actions." There were "perhaps even worse difficulties in trying to decipher what the effects of foundation grants have been."[45] E. Jefferson Murphy's *Creative Philanthropy: Carnegie Corporation and Africa 1953-1973*, which the Corporation commissioned, was in the author's words "to a large extent . . . a descriptive account, leaving it to the reader to reach whatever judgements and assessments he feels may be appropriate."[46] Description is necessary and useful, but evaluation is also required, and an awareness of context is essential. One category of material that should always be treated with caution is plans and statements of intent. Words may never become deeds. Culture Houses were planned for each of the fifty-five districts of Zimbabwe in the 1980s. Each was to have a library, a museum, an oral archive, a hall, arts and crafts, and a printing workshop. S.M. Made and G.C. Motsi, who wrote about the planned Culture Houses, said that the libraries would be focal points for distributing books by mobile van to schools, clinics, and other government institutions.[47] Lucy Atherton (from whom this example comes) pointed out in 1993 that only one had been built and that with aid from Sweden.[48]

The next example shows how the documentation can mislead, unless one is aware of the context. The report of the Northern Nigeria public library service for 1961-63 shows that on 31 March 1963 the Kaduna branch had 5,616 registered readers

---

[44] K.J. Mchombu and K. Miti, "Formulation of National Information Policies in Africa: Some Unlearnt Lessons," *International Information and Library Review* 24 (1992): 169.

[45] Francis X. Sutton, "Foundations and Cultural Development of the Third World," in *Philanthropy and Culture: The International Foundation Perspective*, ed. Kathleen D. McCarthy (Philadelphia: University of Pennsylvania Press for the Rockefeller Foundation, 1984), 138.

[46] E. Jefferson Murphy, *Creative Philanthropy: Carnegie Corporation and Africa 1953-1973* (New York and London: Teachers College Press, 1976), iv.

[47] S.M. Made and G.C. Motsi, "Alternative Ways of Providing Rural Information. Culture Houses: The Zimbabwean Experience," *Zimbabwe Librarian* 18 (1986): 4-6.

[48] Lucy Atherton, "Community Libraries in Zimbabwe," *Information Development* 9 (1993): 40.

and that they borrowed four out of every five books lent.[49] The service for the region had been inaugurated only a decade earlier, so progress had certainly been made. But when one relates the number 5,616 to the size of the population (29,808,659 according to the 1963 census) one realizes that the four out of every five books lent went to readers in the capital who amounted to one out of every 5,308 northern Nigerians.

The Public Library in South Africa: An Evaluative Study (1962) by Theodorus Friis is another example, the kind of bizarre one that South Africa supplied during the long years of apartheid. Friis had been working on the topic for some time. In 1954, after returning from a tour of libraries in Europe and the United States and a spell at the Graduate Library School of the University of Chicago, he had spoken about research to the Natal branch of the South African Library Association. He said that in order to improve the quality of their services they must discover the answers to such questions as "Who uses the public library in South Africa?" Sound scientific research was essential.[50] Friis practised what he preached. He sent out a questionnaire and analyzed the responses from 240 libraries. He looked at the objectives of the public library, referring to the Enoch Pratt Free Library in Baltimore and quoting from publications of the American and British library associations. He gave his personal opinion: that the aim of the public library should be the production of well-educated individuals. He thanked Lester Asheim and others at Chicago and P.C. Coetzee at the University of Pretoria for providing the inspiration for scientific research. Then, on pages 105 and 106, he stated that his study was not concerned with describing or evaluating the library services for the non-European population of South Africa. Thus—almost as an afterthought or one of those limitations best pointed out by authors of scholarly works, before their critics do so for them—Friis mentioned his exclusion of what amounted to more than four-fifths of the population of his country. He did add that the government had expressed its intention of introducing a service for the Bantu

---

[49] Northern Region of Nigeria, Ministry of Information, *Annual Report of the Regional Library Division, Ministry of Information 1961-1963* (Kaduna: Government Printer, 1964), 5-6.

[50] "Branch News: Natal Branch," *SALA Newsletter* 7 (1954): 155.

(the term used at the time by the rulers of South Africa for their black subjects), and that the provision of service for the colored people (the term then applied to South Africans of mixed race) would present no great problem; they had a western background, and therefore, their library service need not differ substantially from that provided for the European.[51]

The early journals such as *WALA News* (as *West African Libraries* was retitled after volume 1) are helpful for record and opinion. Later journals and later articles in foreign journals are often less informative; their editors and authors are aware of the sort of work that is being published elsewhere, particularly in the United States, and interested in producing something similar. The same holds true for some of the higher degree research conducted at American and other universities. An emphasis on applying the methods that had proved so successful for the sciences to other forms of intellectual inquiry was paramount for many years, and different approaches were looked down upon as unscientific and therefore best avoided. According to Herbert Goldhor, dean of the University of Illinois library school in the 1960s and 1970s, the goal of library research should be the formulation of scientific laws: "Until we can state universal generalizations or laws, based on evidence and confirmable by further observations, librarianship will remain an art or a field of practice and will not be a science or discipline."[52] This approach led to exactingly conducted experiments to discover whether annotated booklists resulted in more books being borrowed from small rural public libraries in the American Midwest than unannotated ones: academic exercises indeed. It is not for nothing that Brazilians refer to the Ph.D as the adult's fairy tale.[53]

Susan George is one of many who have pointed out that science is not value-free at all.[54] There is a sense in which nothing is apolitical, not even the weather forecast; when in

[51] Theodorus Friis, *The Public Library in South Africa: An Evaluative Study* (Cape Town/Johannesburg and London: Afrikaanse Pers-Boekhandel and Andre Deutsch, 1962).

[52] Herbert Goldhor, *An Introduction to Scientific Research in Librarianship* (Urbana, Ill.: University of Illinois, Graduate School of Library Science, 1972), 2.

[53] I am indebted to Silas Marques de Oliveira for this piece of information.

[54] Susan George, *Ill Fares the Land: Essays on Food, Hunger and Power* (Harmondsworth, Middlesex: Penguin, 1990), 151.

Beijing in 1989 the author of this book noted that the English language news and weather on Chinese television gave forecasts for Pyongyang, the capital of its ally, North Korea, but not for Seoul, capital of the south.

For Goldhor the major value of doing doctoral research is the discipline that the student experiences. This may suffice for the United States, one of the wealthiest countries in the world, but it is a luxury for less fortunate areas. For Western academics familiar with underdeveloped countries (and it should be pointed out that Goldhor was not at the time he wrote his book) this attitude is difficult to excuse; yet Warren F. Ilchman, writing about American-influenced social science in Southeast Asia, declares: "Research is to the social scientist what prayer is to the religious. The outcome of the research is less important than the activity itself."

Ilchman was writing about social positivism, the "secular faith" which amongst other things believes that "the better the numbers, the greater the likelihood of finding the truth."[55] Positivism was the doctrine of Auguste Comte, the nineteenth century French philosopher, and it is an approach that has had critics as well as adherents: Antonio Gramsci described it as the philosophy of non-philosophers. Obviously someone whose interest in the study of man in society goes beyond the purely academic would be uncomfortable with a range so narrow and an approach that has come to be so centered on quantification and the statistical manipulation of numbers. Supposedly value-free, positivism, like the philanthropism that has given it so much financial backing in the social sciences,[56] accepts the status quo and tries to come up with findings that may lead to amelioration of some of the status quo's defects. It is a distraction that can be relied upon to keep its practitioners safely busy. It is unlikely to lead to fundamental change, and it offers little to students from societies that are desperately in need of change. Paul Streeten uses the phrase "internal brain train" for scholars from developing countries who carry out at home "the kind of irrelevant, esoteric, excessively sophisticated, abstract work that gains prestige in the centers

---

55 Ilchman, "Hybrids," 90, 89.

56 See the papers in Arnove, *Philanthropy.*

of learning of the developed countries."[57]   The irony, as Michael H. Harris points out, is that the tyranny of positivism has been challenged in the social sciences for many years. Deriding the "physics of librarianship" approach, he cites the remark by Anthony Giddens that, while some social scientists still yearn for the arrival of a social-scientific Isaac Newton, not only are they waiting for a train that will not arrive, they are in the wrong station altogether.[58]   Harris calls for historically informed scholarship, cautioning that "any attempt to view the library in isolation from other contemporaneous social activity is inherently distorting and ultimately fruitless."[59]

The reports of library consultants are practical pieces of work, not academic treatises. The best are extremely valuable sources of information and opinion. The problem is that not only are they not widely available, but their very existence may only be known to a few. This was not always the case. In 1929 the Carnegie Corporation of New York printed and distributed the reports on East and Southern Africa which it had commissioned from Milton J. Ferguson and S.A. Pitt (see Chapter 3).[60] Harold Lancour's Carnegie-sponsored visit to West Africa in 1957 was written up as a University of Illinois occasional paper. J.C. Harrison's report on education for librarianship in Ghana was reproduced as an appendix by Evelyn Evans in her account of the Ghana Library Service.[61] The Sharr report on the library needs of Northern Nigeria (see Chapter 7) was published by the regional government in 1963. The British Council made the reports that it sponsored available.

But in the altered political environment of Britain since 1979, the push for privatization and the scaling down of the British

[57] Paul Streeten, "The Limits of Development Research," in Stifel and others, *Social Sciences*, 40.

[58] Cited in Michael H. Harris, "The Dialectic of Defeat: Antimonies in Research in Library and Information Science," *Library Trends* 34 (1986): 521.

[59] Harris, "Dialectic of Defeat," 523.

[60] The two men travelled together, accompanied by their wives. The oddity of two separate reports is explained by Norman Horrocks (Scarecrow Press Vice-President, Editorial), who heard the story from Ralph Munn: the women did not get along.

[61] Evelyn J.A. Evans, *A Tropical Library Service: The Story of Ghana's Libraries* (London: Andre Deutsch, 1964), 145-57.

Council have led to a number of small private consultancy firms being established by librarians and others with overseas experience. Full-time consultants will wish to ensure a continuing supply of paid consultancies. They have different preoccupations from practising librarians, publishers, students, and lecturers and may not appreciate how helpful these up-to-date reports could be to those who do not have the same resources at their disposal. Or, if the consultants are under contract to the World Bank and other bodies to investigate book availability, they may appreciate it only too well. Information given freely by teachers, librarians, publishers, and civil servants in developing countries, and acquired from the staff of sponsoring organizations, is likely to be worth money to Western publishers interested in supplying textbooks that will be paid for out of aid budgets. In such circumstances some consultants may be eager to gather as much and disclose as little information as possible—or, at any rate, as little as possible for free.

More accessible—and equally important—sources of information are the records and files of donors such as Book Aid International. These provide a current picture, although one with a somber perspective.

Chapter 2

Foreign Aid and Its Providers

The greater part of foreign aid for library and information services in British and ex-British Africa has come from Britain and the United States. D.E. Uba, a Nigerian, told the third Afro-Nordic library conference in Finland in 1979 that Britain, more than any other outside government, had aided the development of public library services in the continent.[1] Much of the British aid comes through the British Council and the Overseas Development Administration, which have just completed a scheme to build a new library at Moi University, Kenya, and assist with the development of that university's Faculty of Information Sciences, which admitted its first students in 1988. Other assistance has come from UNESCO, which helped the Makerere library school in the 1960s, and from the Scandinavian countries and Germany.

Examples of international and foreign aid to other parts include UNESCO's help in setting up the library school for students from Francophone Africa in Dakar, Senegal, in the early 1960s, and Canada's paying for the greater part of the cost of the national library building in Abidjan, the Ivory Coast, in the early 1970s. The European Union is also becoming involved in book aid, while the World Bank has become a major provider of books for various levels of education in a number of countries.[2] Robert Davies mentions an estimate that "85 percent of recent World Bank projects in the education sector

[1] D.E. Uba, "Libraries in the African Development Projects: The Problems of the Library Service in Africa," in *Libraries and National Development (Final Report of the Third Afro-Nordic Library Conference, Finland, 3-7 September 1979)* ([Paris]: UNESCO, no date), 180.

[2] See Anthony Read, "International Experiences in Third World Publishing Development with Particular Reference to World Bank Interventions," in *Publishing and Development in the Third World*, ed. Philip G. Altbach (London: Hans Zell, 1992), 307-24.

contain a component dealing with textbooks or supplementary materials at school level or libraries at higher education level."[3] The Bank provided the loan for restocking the libraries of federally-funded universities in Nigeria in the 1990s. It is backing the project to establish a national agricultural library in Ghana. Its role, activities, and influence deserve detailed study.

The British Council

The British Council's library work has been chronicled by Douglas Coombs.[4] The Council was set up in the 1930s "to promote abroad a wider appreciation of British culture and civilisation."[5] When war broke out and the loyalty of the empire assumed a new importance, it was decided to extend its activities to the colonies. Its work was "entirely cultural and non-political," the Colonial Office explained, and "clearly distinct from that of the Ministry of Information, being essentially that of a long-range educative character and not of the nature of propaganda." The colonial secretary, Lord Moyne, felt that the Council could operate in the empire "with great benefit to the local populations and, more especially, to the educated classes."[6]

Informed people in Britain had become concerned about the feelings of educated Africans. Lord Hailey told Margery (later Dame Margery) Perham in 1939 that it was characteristic of the British to feel more at home with "the less intellectual and more primitive type of native people."[7] Hailey, who had compiled the monumental *African Survey* since his retirement from the Indian Civil Service, said he could not count the number of times he had heard his former colleagues regret that they had not seen the necessity of establishing better relations with Indians who had received their education in England. Perham, by then considered one of Britain's leading authorities

3 Robert Davies, "Evaluation of Book Aid Methods Required"[letter], *Library Association Record* 94 (1992): 375.

4 Coombs, *Spreading the Word*.

5 Cited in Frances Donaldson, *The British Council: The First Fifty Years* (London: Jonathan Cape, 1984).

6 J.J. Paskin, Colonial Office, to Chief Secretary, Conference of East African Governors, 6 February 1942, BW7/1, PRO.

7 Lord Hailey to Margery Perham, 11 October 1939, BW2/93, PRO.

on colonial development, had suggested setting up cultural centers in colonial capitals which would provide neutral social ground, where both races could meet and talk without embarrassment. The centers she had in mind would include libraries. She was also interested in bringing selected Africans to England for short visits or to study: "The truth is we shall increasingly need in Africa men and women who can interpret us to their own people as well as vice versa."[8]

Malcolm Guthrie, who spent twelve months traveling on the Council's behalf in East and Central Africa in 1942/43, wrote as follows after his visit to Northern Rhodesia's Northern Province:[9]

> In this territory particularly, partly owing to ideas which spread up from South Africa, partly owing to the lack of anything more interesting to do, there is a tendency for the educated African to use his knowledge in the discussion of grievances, both real and imaginary. He is liable to become a difficult person unless he is given more background. It is becoming fashionable to express strong views about government and the Europeans in general, a tendency which is deplorable in view of the poorness of their grasp of the problems involved. Unless the most promising Africans of this territory are to become the prey of agitators, it is important that they should be given the chance to know what is going on in the world outside, and to realize that their own problems are only a part of those which exist all over the world. With right guidance he can develop into a useful citizen, proud of his association with the British, instead of being taken up with the only facts he knows, chiefly that he has been deprived of his ancestral lands by Europeans who simply want to make money out of them.

The Council opened an office in British West Africa in 1943, but because of shortage of suitable staff and complications such as settler racism in Kenya, it took longer to get going elsewhere.

The American Foundations

Much American aid has come from those legacies of American capitalism, the great private philanthropic foundations. Foremost among these in its support of libraries was the Carnegie Corporation of New York, which Andrew Carnegie established in 1911 with a grant of $25 million, followed two months later with another for $75 million. Having amassed a

---

[8] [Margery Perham], "Cultural Relations between Britain and the African Dependencies," BW2/93, PRO, 8.

[9] Malcolm Guthrie, "Report of an Investigation in the British Dependencies of East and Central Africa," [1944], BW7/1, PRO.

fortune through his own abilities and hard work and through the exploitation of the men who worked in his steel mills, Carnegie concluded it was his duty to give most of it away: the millionaire was the trustee of the poor; the man who died rich died disgraced. Using his revised spelling, he wrote to tell the trustees of his corporation that his chief happiness lay in the "thot [sic] that even after I pass away the welth [sic] that came to me to administer for the good of my fellow men is to continue to benefit humanity for generations untold."[10] Carnegie believed in libraries, though critics pointed out that his own workmen would have been too worn out to use them. His practice was to provide the money for the building, if a municipality would, through taxes, supply the books and undertake to continue maintenance. When a friend wrote to congratulate him for giving sixty-five branch libraries to New York City in 1901, he replied that it was the best bargain he had ever made; the money he had given was a small affair [it was over $5 million] when compared with what he had compelled New York to give. He liked to boast that the sun never set on Carnegie Free Public Libraries.

It seemed fair to say, wrote the Carnegie Corporation's secretary in 1963, that that body had been associated with every major development in library service in the United States and in most parts of the British Commonwealth. It had contributed $33,457,142, although, contrary to the public's image, this had amounted to only 11 percent of the Corporation's grants in the fifty years from 1911 to 1961. Carnegie himself had contributed vast sums in his lifetime (he died in 1919), and these added to what the Corporation gave amounted to $68,333,973. (This does not include what Carnegie and the Carnegie United Kingdom Trust gave in Britain and Ireland). Of this, $5,823,665 or 8.52 percent went to the British Commonwealth (excluding the United Kingdom and the Irish Free State), Canada receiving the lion's share: $3,491,638 or 59.96 percent. British Africa received $894,049 or 15.35 percent of the $5,823,665, and $603,035 or 67.45 percent of this went to South Africa. Thus, of the near $70 million granted by Carnegie for library development outside the United Kingdom and

10 Quoted in Joseph Frazier Wall, *Andrew Carnegie* (New York: Oxford University Press, 1970), 796. Most of the points about Carnegie are taken from this biography.

Ireland up to 1961, less than a million (actually $894,049 or 1.31 percent) went to British Africa, and of this two-thirds went to South Africa. That country, with more whites than anywhere else on the continent, was both more significant and more comprehensible to the Corporation, although a little of the South African grant money was allocated for the commencement of library service to nonwhites.[11]

The Ford Foundation granted some money for library and information services, but on nothing like the scale of the Carnegie Corporation. However, Ford—once described by Dean Rusk as "the fat boy in the philanthropic canoe"[12]—was much bigger. The Rockefeller Foundation gave a little here and there, such as sponsoring a conference on library education in Nairobi in 1963. It also provided a grant to the East African Literature Bureau, which resulted in a literary prize: one winner was James Ngugi, later to become one of East Africa's best known and most controversial writers under the name Ngugi wa Thiong'o.[13] More recently Rockefeller has supported the development of indigenous publishing. *Publishing and Development in the Third World*, the proceedings of a seminar that it hosted at its conference center in Bellagio, Italy, in 1991, is an important contribution to the subject.[14] The Bellagio Publishing Group and the *Bellagio Publishing Network Newsletter* are amongst the outcomes of the seminar.

The Ford Foundation's Francis X. Sutton has pointed out that university development had been the largest category of activity in the Third World for Ford and Carnegie and a significant one for Rockefeller.[15] The foundations are not in competition with each other. In 1962 the principal (later the vice-chancellor) of University College, Ibadan (later the University of Ibadan), was asked by the librarian to approach the foundations for the money with which to extend the university press and hire two additional lecturers for the

---

[11] Florence Anderson, *Carnegie Corporation: Library Program 1911-1961* (New York: Carnegie Corporation of New York, 1963), 24-25, 99-101.

[12] Quoted in Robert F. Arnove, "Foundations and the Transfer of Knowledge," in *Philanthropy and Cultural Imperialism: The Foundations at Home and Abroad*, ed. Robert F. Arnove (Boston: G.K. Hall, 1980), 307.

[13] Charles Richards, "Interview," *African Book Publishing Record* 2 (1976): 161.

[14] *Publishing and Development*, ed. Altbach.

[15] Sutton, "Foundations and Cultural Development," 142.

library school. Ibadan was receiving massive support from Rockefeller, Ford, and Carnegie, and the principal sent this request to Ford. The Ford people knew that the library school had been started with Carnegie money two years earlier and wondered: "Why shouldn't Carnegie stick with this until it has some shape?" They put it back on "Carnegie's plate" after checking and finding that the Corporation planned to continue its support.[16]

People in the aid business and the worlds to which it is connected know each other. There are links between them and universities, government, and business. This interconnectedness is illustrated by the careers of the people who sit on boards and help set their policies. A classic example would be Robert S. McNamara: an executive of the Ford Motor Company from 1946 to 1961, secretary of the US Department of Defense from 1961 to 1968, president of the World Bank from 1968 to 1981. Few are as high-flying as McNamara, but most foundation directors and trustees are well educated, well-to-do, and influential. An appropriate example for this book is Francis Keppel, son of the Carnegie president who oversaw the granting of money for libraries in British Africa in the 1930s. Francis Keppel was dean of education at Harvard University from 1948 to 1962, then US commissioner of education. While at Harvard he served as one of the three Americans on the Carnegie-funded Ashby commission on higher education in Nigeria and later as a member of the provisional council of the new Ahmadu Bello University, Zaria. He was a trustee of the Carnegie Corporation from 1970 to 1979 and in 1980 was appointed to the board of directors of the Canadian International Development Research Centre.[17]

American foundations have a role in extending the influence of the United States and the West. This needs to be stressed because, unlike the British Council, which is quite open about promoting Britain and British culture, the big foundations say they exist for the benefit of all mankind; "to advance human welfare" is the phrase on the title page of Ford annual reports.

---

16 Memo to D. Kingsley from F. Champion Ward, May 15, 1962; memo to F.X. S[utton] from F. Champion Ward, June 13, 1962. Ford Foundation Archives, PA63-01.

17 *Who's Who in America 1986-87* (Wilmette, Ill.: Marquis Who's Who, 1986) and other sources.   ·

Robert F. Arnove has criticized them as follows:[18]

> Foundations like Carnegie, Rockefeller and Ford have a corrosive influence on a democratic society; they represent relatively unregulated and unaccountable concentrations of power and wealth which buy talent, promote causes, and, in effect, establish an agenda of what merits society's attention. They serve as "cooling out" agencies, delaying and preventing more radical, structural change. They help maintain an economic and political order, international in scope, which benefits the ruling-class interests of philanthropists and philanthropoids—a system which . . . has worked against the interests of minorities, the working class, and Third World peoples.

Charitable Aid and Book Aid International

Charity is a word with uncomfortable connotations, and books donated to libraries for free have aroused mixed feelings over the years. When John Harris arrived to establish the library at the newly-founded University College, Ibadan, in 1948, he found seventy large wooden crates of books before him, a gift from well-meaning organizations in Britain: "There were works on sanitary engineering designed for England in the nineteenth century; there were two volumes of a five-volume work on the topography of Wales in 1820; there were books of essays on long dead ecclesiastical issues of Victorian England; there were twelve copies of Morley's *Life of Cobden*, and possibly the least useful of the whole collection, twenty-five copies of a pamphlet on *How to win the war*, addressed to the Polish people, and in the Polish language."[19]

The Sierra Leone Library Board states that there are times when it is inundated by books that cannot be used at all: United States publishers who send surpluses are the worst offenders.[20] The consultant Julie Carpenter and her colleagues referred to the "high proportion of largely irrelevant donated books taking up shelf space which would otherwise be empty" in Zambian secondary schools and teacher-training institutions.[21] The librarian of the International Bauxite Association,

---

[18] Arnove, *Philanthropy*, 1.

[19] John Harris, *Ibadan University Library: Some Notes on Its Birth and Growth* (Ibadan: Ibadan University Press, 1968), 15.

[20] Sierra Leone Government, *Report of the Sierra Leone Library Board October 1987 - June 1990* (Freetown: Government Printing Department, 1990), 3.

[21] Julie Carpenter and others, "The Books Sector in Zambian Education: A Study Prepared for the Delegate of the Commission of the European Communities and the Government of the Republic of Zambia," 1990.

Kingston, Jamaica, summed up one big donor as "another out-dated, well-intentioned failure, and an example of British arrogance and ignorance which believes that books that are dirty, well-decorated with others' scribbles, etc., and mostly irrelevant, are good enough for the developing countries . . . . Such cheek!"[22]

The big donor is Book Aid International (formerly the Ranfurly Library Service), which supplied 637,879 volumes in 1992, 80 percent of them to Commonwealth countries in Africa.[23] The organization was started in 1954 by the countess of Ranfurly and her husband, then governor and commander-in-chief of the Bahamas. Lady Ranfurly sent teachests of books free of freight charges to the outer islands. Looking back on this work over twenty years later, the Bahamian newspaper publisher Sir Etienne Dupuch said that the countess represented "the qualities that are finest in the British race, the spirit that sent young men to distant outposts of the world to light a candle in dark areas of the human family."[24]

On returning home in 1957 the Ranfurlys were prevailed upon by Lord Boyd and others to continue to expand the service. Always well-connected,[25] they secured Prince Philip, duke of Edinburgh, as Patron, and Lord Boyd, Lord Amory, and Air Chief Marshall Sir John Slessor as Council members. They acquired "two terrible little rooms" in the basement of the English Speaking Union in Mayfair and set to work. "The original rules were that, because of the vast need for books in less lucky countries, we should forward all books in good

---

22 Shirley Davis, "Outdated Intentions Insult Developing Nations" [letter], *Library Association Record* 94 (1992): 244.

23 In addition to the specific references that follow, sources on which this account of Book Aid International are based include interviews with David Membrey, deputy director, 10 August 1993, and Ard Jongsma, International Campus Book Link, 4 August 1993; Book Aid promotional leaflets; Book Aid files; David Membrey, "The Modern Ranfurly" [letter], *Library Association Record* 94 (1992): 375; and a feature by Book Aid staff under various headings in the *Library Association Record* 95 (1993): 32-33.

24 Sir Etienne Dupuch, "Past Governors' Wives," *The Tribune* [Nassau], 12 February 1977, [page reference not recorded on BAI newspaper cutting].

25 For plenty of examples see *To War with Whitaker: The Wartime Diaries of the Countess of Ranfurly 1939-1945* (London: Heinemann, 1994). Whitaker was George Gibbon Whitaker, her husband's valet, who once remarked: "The difference between His Lordship and me is that he was brought up and I was dragged up. I've had to educate myself in every respect."

condition—books on all subjects, for all age groups, to be distributed and made available to whole communities and only evil books and those in tatty condition be discarded."[26] Rotary Club members in Britain and elsewhere helped as did volunteers. More spacious premises were acquired and a permanent staff built up. Sir Charles Troughton, former head of the British Council, took over the chairmanship from the earl, later handing it on to Julian Smith, a director of W.H. Smith, the largest bookselling firm in Britain. Evelyn J.A. Evans served as a consultant in the 1970s and 1980s, as did K.C. Harrison, former Westminster city librarian. Evans made a number of visits and distributed forms so that recipients could evaluate the usefulness or otherwise of books supplied.

By 1994 Book Aid had twenty-three full-time and six part-time staff, including five qualified librarians. It is a professionally run, registered charity that raises money from governments, trusts, companies, and individuals. The Overseas Development Administration has provided money since 1968, but the amount has never exceeded 15 percent of income.[27] The Beit Trust (after Alfred Beit, the gold and diamond magnate who was a friend of Cecil Rhodes and one of his trustees) gives money for Malawi, Zambia, and Zimbabwe. The European Union is giving a grant to fund services to Kenya, Tanzania, and Uganda for three years. Barclays Bank is supporting the International Campus Book Link, which helps: (1) to fill gaps in the journal holdings of university libraries in a number of African countries, and (2) to pass on donated current volumes of journals such as *The Lancet* to libraries whose lack of foreign exchange makes it impossible for them to keep up their subscriptions. Book Aid provides detailed guidelines to librarians and others throughout Britain who supply books, which must be in reasonable physical condition and reasonably up-to-date. Computer studies titles, for example, must be no more than five years old. Obviously some inappropriate material is received, and changes in the supply and demand of wastepaper mean that Book Aid must now pay to get rid of this instead of its being a source of income as hitherto.

---

[26] "A Note to All Members of the R.L.S. Council from H. Ranfurly, 26.11.1992," Book Aid Archive file, BAI.

[27] Sara Harrity, " 'Extracting the Gold' from Book Surpluses," *Logos* 5 (1994): 154.

Selection is done in the London warehouse by Book Aid and by librarians from some of the overseas institutions that receive the books. Staff members from the Ghana Library Board and the Namibian Union of Students each spent three months with Book Aid in 1993 under a fellowship scheme sponsored by the Nuffield Foundation. Harare and Bulawayo Libraries in Zimbabwe each pay travel and subsistence expenses for one of their librarians to come to London for short selection visits.[28] Akwa Ibom, one of the new states brought into being by the Nigerian government in its 1991 redivision of the country into smaller internal units, sent two librarians to London to select Book Aid material for its newly established college of education and polytechnic and for the state library headquarters. The subsistence expenses for their four-week visit in 1992 were paid by Akwa Ibom, the air fares by Akwa Ibom and the British Council.[29] Book Aid distributes detailed book requirement forms, which ask institutions to state their priorities and to evaluate previous consignments. Members of staff also make a number of overseas visits each year to ensure that books and journals are reaching readers as intended and to evaluate their usefulness.

Increasingly Book Aid is involved in the provision of new publications. It purchased books to the value of £300,000 in 1993.[30] Recent projects include the supply of 110,000 primary school English and mathematics textbooks to Belize, paid for by the European Union. The Belize Ministry of Education selected the titles, which were produced for the Caribbean market by British publishers. African publishers receive backing through the Intra African Book Support Scheme. The Netherlands government pays for the provision of African-published children's books to libraries and schools in other parts of the continent. Comic Relief, the fund-raising charity, pays for the provision of African-published texts to universities.

---

28 . . . , City of Harare, to BAI, 7 August 1992, Zimbabwe—Completed Special Requests A Numbers, BAI; Bulawayo Public Library, *Seventh Triennial Report 1989-1992* (Bulawayo: Bulawayo Public Library, 1992), 3.

29 "Ranfurly Library Service: A Report of the Four Week Book Selection by . . . ," 1992, Nigeria—Completed Special Requests file, BAI.

30 Harrity, "Extracting the Gold," 154.

For a whole range of reasons it is generally a problem for one African country to acquire books from another. Indeed "well nigh impossible" was the summing up of the Sierra Leone Library Board, which found it easier to acquire them from Britain.[31] This situation deprives Africans of much good quality material. A Book Aid tie-up with the African Books Collective (ABC) is one attempt to circumvent this. ABC is an initiative by a number of African publishers, with aid from Ford and Rockefeller, the Swedish International Development Authority, the Norwegian Agency for International Development, the Canadian Organization for Development through Education (CODE), and the Commonwealth Foundation.[32] The aim is to promote African publications in Commonwealth countries outside the continent, in North America and in Europe. Multiple copies of English-language children's books, academic books, creative writing, and general interest titles are shipped to ABC's office in Oxford, where catalogs are prepared and mailed to existing and potential customers. Money raised by Book Aid and by ABC sends some of these books back to Africa to places they would never reach otherwise.

To what extent do the criticisms of donated books apply to Book Aid International and to other contemporary programs? "The fact remains," Robert Davies maintains, "that most of what is given away by the voluntary schemes is something that someone, somewhere doesn't want."[33] He suggests a study to compare the impact of a sample of donated books with a sample provided under a development scheme or through a nationally funded project. Book Aid does devote a great deal of effort to various forms of evaluation. But, as one of its distributors points out, a teacher in charge of a library in a rural area of Zimbabwe needs books so badly that he or she would be unlikely to offer criticism—constructive or otherwise—for fear it might jeopardize future donations.[34] Another dimension becomes obvious from the acknowledgement by a librarian in Zimbabwe

---

[31] . . . , Sierra Leone Library Board, 22 April 1992, to BAI, Sierra Leone General file, BAI.

[32] African Books Collective Ltd. catalogs.

[33] Davies, "Evaluation of Book Aid," 375.

[34] . . . , 4 May 1992, to BAI, Zimbabwe General file, BAI.

that his twenty-seven staff members are completely dependent on what Book Aid supplies for their continuing employment.[35]

Published criticisms such as that of the librarian of the International Bauxite Association, Jamaica, draw rejoinders: the director of the Anambra State Library Board, Nigeria, retorted that his readers were very happy with the books they received.[36] Book Aid's own files are full of positive responses from institutions in many countries. John Harris, who learned about unsuitable donations the hard way at Ibadan in 1948, went on to admit that valuable material did come later and that it was the library's own fault, if items were accepted that did not fit its acquisition policy.[37] A professionally organized book donation program with built-in evaluation procedures can undoubtedly supply much needed valuable material. A question that does arise, however, is whether such a supply is in danger of becoming a permanent substitute for action for some in Africa charged with the responsibility of providing financial support for their own library and information services.

[35] . . . , 14 July 1992, to BAI, Zimbabwe Completed Special Requests—A Numbers file, BAI.

[36] Chris N. Ekweozoh, "Vital Ranfurly Service" [letter], *Library Association Record* 94 (1992): 451.

[37] Harris, *Ibadan University Library*, 16.

Chapter 3

The Kenya (Carnegie) Circulating Libraries and the McMillan Memorial Library, Nairobi

Dr. F.P. Keppel, president of the Carnegie Corporation of New York, and James Bertram, the secretary, made a visit of inspection to east and southern Africa in 1927. In Kenya they were told about the need for library services. One of the Europeans they spoke to was Carolyn Cox (Mrs. J. Raffles Cox). She later spoke to Mr. Orr, the Church of Scotland minister, and to Mr. Shaw, the manager of Standard Bank, Nairobi, and wrote to tell Dr. Keppel that one point they were quite clear about was that, if Carnegie libraries were to be set up, every consideration must be given, not only to the European population, but also to the Asians and Africans.[1] However, nonwhites were excluded from consideration by the East Africa Women's League, which soon put Cox in her place. This organization, affiliated with the Society for Overseas Settlement of British Women, was established in 1917 to press for the vote for women (the vote was about to be given to every British male of European origin in the colony). Its long-term aim was to study and act on "all matters affecting the welfare and happiness of women and children of all races in East Africa."[2] Its immediate concerns during the 1920s included the servants, "whose indiscipline, laziness, insolence, and general misbehaviour . . . was worse than ever . . . . The native had got out of hand."[3] Another was the absolute necessity of censoring

---

[1] Carolyn Cox to F.P. Keppel, 8 December 1927. This and all other letters and Kenya library reports cited in this chapter are, unless otherwise stated, from the Kenya Colony—Library Development file, CCNY archives.

[2] East Africa Women's League, *Sixty Years: 1917-1977* (Nairobi: East Africa Women's League, 1977), 2.

[3] "Problem of Native Domestic Servants. Discussion by Ruiru Branch of E.A.W.L.," *East African Standard*, 12 February 1927, 10.

films, because "as long as the coloured races are allowed to see pictures in which the white races are degraded we are not only risking the security of our homes but slowly and surely sowing the seeds of the downfall of the white races."[4] The League excluded African and other nonwhite women from membership until several months before Kenyan independence in 1963.[5] Ailsa Turner, its president from 1925 until 1940 (and one of its enthusiasts for registration and censorship), wrote to Keppel to say that people were very much of the same opinion about the library scheme apart from Mrs. Raffles Cox, "but she has nothing to do with the Women's League or anything else in particular & it does not appear that anyone else shares her views."[6] Mrs. Turner and her husband were to play a significant part in the provision of library services for the white population of Kenya in the 1930s. He was a onetime lieutenant colonel who had served in the Boer War and in the South West Africa and East Africa fronts of the 1914-18 war. In between he had worked in the Transvaal. Since 1924 he had been commissioner for the Union of South Africa in British East Africa.[7]

On 24 April 1928 the Kenya colonial secretary, Sir Edward Denham, Colonel and Mrs. Turner, the Church of Scotland minister, and the Church of England dean of Nairobi submitted a letter in which they proposed a scheme for extending the circulation of books throughout the colony to "the world's Pioneers in library work."[8] The scheme had been unanimously approved at a meeting at which all sections of the community had been represented. The sections were listed. They included the government, represented by the colonial secretary; the African community, represented by the deputy chief native

---

[4] "The Electors in Nairobi. Women's League Hears Three Candidates. Daylight Saving Difficulties," *East African Standard*, 5 February 1927, 40.

[5] Elspeth Huxley told Margery Perham in 1943 that the League was about to repeal a clause in its constitution restricting membership to European women (*Race and Politics in Kenya* [London: Faber and Faber, 1944], 206). Richard Frost, who consulted the League's minute book, says its constitution was not altered until 1963 (Frost, *Race Against Time*, 198-200).

[6] Ailsa Turner to Keppel, 3 March 1928.

[7] *Who Was Who, 1971-1980* (London: Adam and Charles Black, 1981), 810. Turner was born in 1879 and died in 1972. Ailsa Turner, his first wife, died in 1949.

[8] Sir Edward Denham and others to the president, Carnegie Corporation, 24 April 1928.

commissioner (who was, of course, British); and the Women's League (which was, of course, white). There were a number of club libraries in existence already, ranging in size from eight thousand volumes at the Nairobi Club to fifty at the Women's League Library at Makuyu, near Thika. What was wanted was "the welding together of the separate and distinct library units of the Colony into such a well-articulated and smoothly working whole that the book needs of every citizen may be promptly filled, that the book in demand may go, without delay, where it will be of use." A comparison was made with California; the main difference, they stated, was that their scheme would not be maintained from public funds for the time being at least. Kenya was "a Colony in the making," and the demands on government were heavy. They asked for £13,500 (equivalent to $67,500 at the time) to be spread over three years. This would cover a librarian's salary, transport, books, and clerical help. They gave the population figures for the colony as a whole and the nonnative figures for the towns and some of the country districts. Kenya's population was expressed as follows by Margery (later Dame Margery) Perham in *The Times* in 1931: "about 15,000 European settlers . . . twice as many Indians, and nearly 200 times as many natives."[9] The letter from the Kenya establishment to the Carnegie Corporation mentioned that the vast majority of natives were still "quite illiterate."[10]

Keppel said it would give him great pleasure to help, but he felt the need for professional advice.[11] The Corporation had arranged for Milton J. Ferguson, state librarian of California, and S.A. Pitt, city librarian of Glasgow, to visit east and southern Africa and report. They arrived in Kenya in December 1928. In his report Ferguson stated that the Denham letter was a fair and intelligent statement of the case. The problem was how best to bring books to a small number of white persons and, to a lesser degree, to a larger group of Asians, all scattered over a wide sweep of country. As for the natives, while they were, "no doubt, making very appreciable progress toward

[9] Reprinted in Margery Perham, *Colonial Sequence: 1930 to 1949: A Chronological Commentary upon British Colonial Policy Especially in Africa* (London: Methuen, 1967), 37.

[10] Denham and others, 24 April 1928.

[11] Keppel to Denham, 2 June 1928.

civilization, it will be many years before they will require a considerable amount of library service." The whites were in danger of "intellectual deterioration," if their reading was confined to current fiction. They had book clubs, but there was no library structure of any kind. However, the widow of the settler Sir Northrup McMillan was erecting a library in Nairobi in memory of her husband, and this could serve as the headquarters of the scheme to bring books to rural areas. Ferguson recommended that the Corporation grant £12,000 ($60,000), spreading it over five years, on condition that the colony adopt a library plan that would "embrace the principles now fairly well established," hire a competent librarian as director, and agree to continue on the service after the grant would expire. The American Library Association's minimum standard was a dollar per capita for library support, which if followed would give the European population about $13,000, but he was recommending more, because a basic book collection would have to be built up and because "service in a way not herein indicated should in all reason be given to the Indians and others through proper channels."[12] Pitt also recommended that the Corporation make a grant. If, after three years of service to Europeans, the Corporation was encouraged by results to go further, then the needs of non-Europeans might receive "close and sympathetic attention."[13]

The Corporation decided to grant $15,000 (£3,000), to be spread out over three years, "primarily for the purchase of books for a central library for the Colony," upon receipt of evidence that the scheme would be under professional direction and that the budget would include substantial support from local sources.[14] This was despite the misgivings of its secretary, James Bertram, who had seen little resemblance between Kenya and California during his visit.[15] The Turners were

---

12 *Report of Mr. Milton J. Ferguson on the Libraries in the Union of South Africa, Rhodesia and Kenya Colony* (New York: Carnegie Corporation of New York, 1929), 32-33.

13 S.A. Pitt, *Memorandum: Libraries in the Union of South Africa, Rhodesia and Kenya Colony* (New York: Carnegie Corporation of New York, 1929), 45.

14 "Kenya Colony: Library Aid," [18 December 1929]; J.M.R. to R.B. Turner, 20 October 1930, and enclosure "II. P. Kenya Colony: Library Development."

15 James Bertram, "Memorandum on 'Libraries for Kenya Colony' with Reference to Application of April 24, 1928," 11 December 1929.

disappointed that the grant was not larger but were still, of course, very grateful.[16] Keppel wished that the Corporation was able to give more, but its funds were limited and the British Empire was "a terribly big place."[17]

The Library Service

Colonel Turner told the members of his Kenya Rural Library Scheme Committee that Keppel had confirmed that the grant was intended to assist European libraries only.[18] A Carnegie summary of the scheme, dated 24 July 1930, states that all new books bought with Carnegie and other money would be distributed from a central depot in Nairobi to "all European libraries in Colony linked up with organization."[19] The depot would be managed by a librarian and an assistant. The number of books each library would obtain would depend on the amount of money its members wished to subscribe. Eight volumes would be supplied for every pound. These would be exchanged every three or four months so that a library subscribing twenty pounds could expect to receive between five and six hundred books a year.[20] An agreement had been reached with Lady McMillan that her McMillan Memorial Library would house the scheme's depot; in return the scheme's librarians would also manage her library.

With its board of trustees and chief librarian working hard to supply books to the white population, the Kenya (Carnegie) Circulating Libraries proved a great success. "You will be glad to see how eagerly the people of this little colony have seized the opportunities made available by the generosity of the Corporation," the chairman of the board wrote to the Carnegie secretary in 1933.[21] The chairman was the director of education for Kenya (and before that for the Transvaal), H.S. Scott. The chief librarian was B. Barton-Eckett, former librarian of the county of Durham in England and before that of the county of

---

16 Ailsa Turner to Keppel, 15 March 1930.

17 Keppel to Mrs. R.B. Turner [Ailsa Turner], 15 April 1930.

18 R.B. Turner to all members of the Kenya Rural Library Scheme Committee.

19 "Kenya Library Scheme," 24 July 1930.

20 B. Barton-Eckett, "Terms and Conditions Governing the Establishment of Branch Libraries."

21 H.S. Scott to R.M. Lester, 22 March 1933.

Dorset. He arrived in Kenya in November 1931. Turner would
have preferred someone from South Africa, because then the
scheme would not have to pay the cost of long leave and sea
passage to Britain.[22] But southern Africa had few librarians
who were both professionally qualified and experienced, and
neither M.M. Stirling of Germiston in the Transvaal nor Dugald
Niven (experienced but not qualified) of Bulawayo, Southern
Rhodesia, were interested. The secretary of the Carnegie
United Kingdom Trust, Colonel Mitchell, was approached and
recommended Barton-Eckett, who was appointed.

Barton-Eckett was delighted with the progress made in his
first two and a half years: thirty-four centers, he told the
Carnegie president, most of them in places that had had no
service before.[23] By 1940 the number of participating centers in
Kenya was forty-nine, including eleven government schools for
white children. Nine centers in Uganda also participated.[24]
Barton-Eckett would have liked to include Tanganyika in his
little empire, but the Carnegie Corporation said no. Germany's
colonies had been taken away after World War I and
Tanganyika allocated to Britain under League of Nations
mandate. A mandated territory, being neither a colony nor a
dominion, was technically outside the scope of the
Corporation's terms of reference.

Nairobi was by far the biggest center. The circulating library
was housed in the McMillan Library, though administered as
part of the Kenya (Carnegie) scheme. At the ceremony for the
laying of the foundation stone in 1929 one of the speakers had
referred to the late Sir Northrup McMillan's wish "to provide
a place where tired minds could find refreshment."[25] At the
opening ceremony in 1931 Lord Delamere, the settlers' leader,
said that "nothing has been more wanted in this Town than a
public library . . . no city or country can really advance without
the aid of good books." According to the director of education

---

[22] R.B. Turner to Keppel, 15 May 1930.

[23] Barton-Eckett to Keppel, 26 April 1934.

[24] McMillan Memorial Library: Headquarters of the Kenya (Carnegie)
Circulating Libraries, "Report of the Board of Trustees and the Ninth Annual
Report of the Librarian: 1st January to 31st December, 1940," 4. The libraries are
listed on pages 6 and 7 and when counted come to a slightly different total.

[25] "The McMillan Memorial Library. Foundation Stone Laid," *East African
Standard*, 8 June 1929, 15.

the library should be "of real value to every member of the European community and enable the problems of Kenya to be approached in perhaps a spirit of more scientific appreciation and with a spirit of wider knowledge so gathered from experience of . . . other countries and of old times."[26] The McMillan Library was for reference and reading, not for circulation, and Lady McMillan supplied several thousand books; of special significance, in Barton-Eckett's opinion, were the facsimiles of Burns, Swinburne, and Shelley. There was a complete set of Curtis's *North American Indian*, Brinkley's ten volumes on Japanese life and art, a limited edition of Sir Richard Burton's *Arabian Nights*, and sets of Victor Hugo, Goethe, and Schiller, "books of which any library might well be proud."[27] There was the 1929 edition of the *Encyclopaedia Britannica*, presented by Dr. Jex Blake in memory of Denys Finch-Hatton (the friend of Karen Blixen, who would later write *Out of Africa*).[28] The furnishings and equipment were as lavish as he had ever seen in a public building: "A finer gift to the Colony it is impossible to imagine."[29]

The stock of the Kenya (Carnegie) Circulating Libraries was less highbrow. Barton-Eckett's "great fight" was to get his clientele to look on the library more as an educational service and less as the cheapest way of getting hold of the latest best-sellers advertised in the newspapers from home.[30] In this he was echoing a common concern of those responsible for the fee-charging whites-only library services of southern Africa. The 1911 annual report of the Bulawayo Public Library in Southern Rhodesia, for example, states that "221 Solid Works and 204 fiction" were acquired during the year. The 1912 report mentions the chairman's pleasure at being able to call attention to the percentage of books of a "solid nature" read, a percentage more

---

[26] "Opening of McMillan Memorial Library. Tributes to Memory of a Great Pioneer and Settler. Ceremony Performed by His Excellency," *East African Standard*, 20 June 1931, 20.

[27] McMillan Memorial Library: Headquarters of the Kenya (Carnegie) Circulating Libraries, "Report and Programme of Development" [1932].

[28] McMillan Memorial Library: Headquarters of the Kenya (Carnegie) Circulating Libraries, "First Annual Report of the Librarian: January 1st–December 31st 1932."

[29] Barton-Eckett to Keppel, 26 April 1934.

[30] Barton-Eckett to Keppel, 26 April 1934.

"wholesome" than that of any town in the Union of South
Africa other than Capetown.[31]   Barton-Eckett told the
Carnegie president that the population of Kenya Colony was
very largely composed of one social class: "the public school-
cum ex Army Officer type, people of a good academic education
to whom reading now-a-days is almost wholly a social
pastime."[32]

The number of registered borrowers rose from 1,431 in 1932 to
1,581 in 1934, a small increase unless one takes into account the
fact that many borrowers represented households. The book
stock nearly doubled during this period (from 5,143 to 9,724
volumes), while the number of books borrowed more than
doubled (from 33,763 to 71,564). The average issue per borrower
rose from twenty-five to forty-five. The income from
subscriptions went up from £544 to £679.[33] The government of
Kenya was giving two hundred pounds a year to the Circulating
Libraries and three hundred to the McMillan, while the
municipality of Nairobi was giving five hundred a year to the
McMillan.[34] The original Carnegie grant to the Circulating
Libraries was one thousand pounds (five thousand dollars) a
year for three years. A supplementary grant continued this for
another two years. The cessation of the three hundred pounds a
year that Lady McMillan had given the McMillan Library for
three years and the uncertainty about what would happen
when the supplementary grant would expire worried Colonel
Turner. On 21 April 1934 he wrote to Keppel to say that he
would like to get rid of his chief librarian: Barton-Eckett was
being paid too much money and his social background and
morals were not all that one would desire.

Turner versus Barton-Eckett

Using the stationery of the Muthaiga Country Club and
marking the letter confidential, Turner told Keppel that
Barton-Eckett was in some ways good but in others

---

[31] Bulawayo Public Library, *Sixteenth Annual Report: Being for Year 1st January to
31st December 1911 . . .* (Bulawayo, no date), 1; *Seventeenth Annual Report: Being for
Year 1st January to 31st December 1912 . . .* (Bulawayo, no date), 3.

[32] Barton-Eckett to Keppel, 26 April 1934.

[33] Kenya (Carnegie) Circulating Libraries, "Review of the Period 1931-34."

[34] Barton-Eckett to Keppel, 26 April 1934.

disappointing.[35] He had profited from the ignorance of new members of the committee of management that the trustees appointed. His head had swollen, his manner become arrogant. While at Durham he had become involved with a female assistant, and this had caused trouble with his wife. He had promised Colonel Mitchell that this extramarital involvement would cease but had not honored his promise. He had imported his "No. 2 lady" into the colony, passing her off as his wife, and the deception only became public knowledge after eighteen months. To complicate matters further she had given birth to a son! Against Turner's judgement his co-trustees had agreed to extend Barton-Eckett's contract by another year, which meant that he would be around until November 1935 unless he became quite impossible.

In coming to their decision the trustees bore in mind the stipulation in the original Carnegie grant that the scheme must be professionally directed. Turner asked Keppel if the Corporation would be satisfied with the lady who had worked as their assistant librarian for the last two and a half years. This was Priscilla M. Allen, who had accompanied her father, a Church of England clergyman, to Kenya in 1931. She had a degree from Oxford, a library diploma from University College London, and library and other working experience. Another possibility—and this would save a lot of money—would be to replace Barton-Eckett with an ex-government senior official, retired on pension and willing to accept three to four hundred pounds a year and no additional privileges. (Barton-Eckett was making eight hundred, Turner said, if one took his leave and paid passages to and from England into account). It would not be difficult to find "a gentleman who is literally minded [sic] and well read with the right broad outlook regarding the Standard of literature we all want to encourage in the Colony and who

---

[35] The use of Muthaiga stationery was ironic, given the fame of the club for the sexual escapades of some of its members. James Fox, *White Mischief* (London: Jonathan Cape, 1982), an account of the murder in 1941 of one of its habitues (the 22nd earl of Errol), gives details of the aristocratic high spirits of some of its members and visitors. One, in protest against the suggestion that Jews be admitted, set fire to the piano. The prince of Wales was there in 1928 and, assisted by his partner, threw the gramophone records to whose music they had been dancing through the ballroom windows. Colonel Turner would hardly have approved, but one imagines that he would have found less to complain about in royalty than in Barton-Eckett.

would be more suitable, from a social point of view, than the present holder of the post." Turner hoped Keppel would forgive him for bringing up what might appear to be minor points, "but you, I am sure, appreciate that these points are to *us* of much importance."[36]

Barton-Eckett knew that Turner was out to get him. He too wrote to Keppel. Using library stationery and also marking his letter confidential, he devoted eight pages to giving "some little account" of the library and himself. He said there was friction between the representatives of the Kenya (Carnegie) Circulating Libraries and the McMillan Library. The Turners, the very people who should have been most helpful, had proved an obstacle to progress. They maintained that the McMillan was benefiting at the expense of the Carnegie scheme, whereas in fact it was the other way around. Fortunately the other trustees knew well that the Turners were "notorious mischief makers."

He had no doubt but that an application would be made for a continuation of the grant. He knew that Carnegie assistance could not continue indefinitely, and suggested that any future grant should be made only on condition that the Nairobi municipality or the Kenya government would undertake responsibility for the combined scheme, before any such grant would expire. At present the library was nobody's child. Barton-Eckett would prefer Nairobi to take it over, under their powers as a public library authority, with the government contribution and the branch subscriptions maintaining the service outside the capital.

He also suggested that any future grant should be made only on condition that the services of the chief librarian be retained at a salary not less than that originally offered. He had given up one of the best positions in the library profession in England on the distinct understanding that the Kenya job would be permanent. Not only that, he had accepted a salary of six hundred and fifty pounds (eight hundred, including home leave and cost of passages, was the figure given to Keppel by Turner) only to discover that it had previously been offered to Stirling and Niven at eight hundred. He loved the country; he was very happy there; he would be extremely sorry to say "Goodbye to

---

[36] Ralph Turner [R.B. Turner] to Keppel, 21 April 1934.

Kenya." But with the financial position being so uncertain he was bound to consider himself, and if Keppel knew of any other scheme, would he please keep him in mind? Any part of the world would do, even the arctic regions, though he knew the Corporation had sent E.A. Savage (the Edinburgh city librarian) to the West Indies to report, and if a librarian was needed there, Barton-Eckett's experience was just the type to be of use.[37]

"Compare with Turner" is written on Barton-Eckett's letter in the Carnegie archives. The file contains no record of a reply to Barton-Eckett, but it does contain Keppel's short reply to Turner. You seem to be having more than your share of difficulties, he commiserated, but no doubt things will work out in the end. Miss Allen's qualifications were perfectly adequate should they wish to appoint her—people in direct contact with the situation were in a much better position than the Corporation to decide these things.[38] On 17 July 1934 John M. Moore, the chairman of the board of trustees, wrote to inquire whether the stipulation about professional direction could be dispensed with. Their chief librarian was "technically quite satisfactory," but because of a shortage of money they were trying to obtain an equally well-qualified librarian who would work for less. Should this not prove possible, and "now that the Library is established as a going concern" and has been "organised on proper lines by an expert," the trustees wanted to know if the Carnegie contributions would be affected were they to appoint a nonlibrarian, for instance, a retired official on pension who would be glad to work for less?[39] Keppel's answer was that the Corporation was more interested in the spirit than the letter of its grant. He knew of cases where a person without previous library experience or training had proved successful, but he knew of more where such persons had not. In the library's own interest he thought it would be best to find someone with at least one of the two requirements: professional training or practical experience. What about a woman, he asked? Women were directing some of the largest public libraries in the United States, and directing them very satisfactorily: "A woman can be

[37] Barton-Eckett to Keppel, 26 April 1934.

[38] Keppel to Turner, 28 May 1934.

[39] John M. Moore to the president, Carnegie Corporation, 17 July 1934.

obtained at a salary very much lower than that of a man with the same qualifications."[40]

Later in 1934 the mantle of chair of the trustees fell on Turner, who described it as "no light garment to carry in these days of difficulties, present and to come." He told Keppel that they were trying to take his advice and find a "Lady Chief Librarian," because it was obvious that they could not afford to maintain their present man. The "lady assistant," who was professionally qualified, was adequate at what she was doing but would not fill the bill for the senior post.[41] She was earning three hundred pounds a year at the time and, forty years later, described herself as being very well paid for the times: able to live in a good hotel (the Fairview or the Grosvenor), run a car, and really do everything she wanted. She also mentioned that they had hoped that the service, having been tried out on Europeans, would later be extended to all races.[42]

Aftermath

Barton-Eckett survived, continuing on until his retirement in 1951. All his letters and reports indicate pleasure at a job well done. His first report, for example, mentions the happy coincidence by which the two aspects of library service—reference and lending—came together so that Kenya was able to begin at a point that older countries had only reached after years of wasteful isolation and independence.[43] But service to Africans? Barton-Eckett was not someone whom Colonel Turner would call a gentleman, and his "No. 2 lady" would hardly have been welcome in Mrs. Turner's Women's League, but he resembled the Turners in at least one thing, lack of interest in the needs of the people who, as Margery Perham put it, outnumbered the whites of Kenya by two hundred to one.

The Carnegie Corporation made a third grant in November 1935, emphasizing that this would be the last. It was for $15,000, to be paid in decreasing amounts over four years. The

---

[40] Keppel to Moore, 21 August 1934.

[41] Turner to Keppel, 1 November 1934.

[42] "Footsteps in Librarianship: Miss Priscilla M. Allen Talks to *Maktaba* about Her Past Experiences . . . ," *Maktaba* 4 (1977): 29.

[43] McMillan Memorial Library: Headquarters of the Kenya (Carnegie) Circulating Libraries, "Report and Programme of Development."

1. Three library pioneers in Africa: B. Barton-Eckett, Jessie Carnell in youth, and Ethel Fegan in later life.

2. Ethel Fegan and the members of the Benin Library Committee, 1941.

3. Sir Alan Burns, governor of the Gold Coast, receiving homage from a chief at the Kumasi Durbar, 12 December 1946.

4. Early days of the Gold Coast Library Board's mobile service.

5. The Zanzibar book exhibition, 1955: Charles Richards, Sir Khalifa bin Harub, sultan of Zanzibar and—looking over his shoulder—the British resident, Sir Henry Potter.

6. Sir Evelyn Baring, governor of Kenya, and Charles Richards at an East African Literature Bureau display, Nairobi.

7. The West African Library Association's annual conference was held at Ibadan in 1956. Front row, commencing third from left: Kalu Okorie, John Harris, Jessie Carnell, George Pitcher (a graduate of Ethel Fegan's library school), and Evelyn Evans.

8. The opening of the Padmore Research Library, Accra, 30 June 1961: Kwame Nkrumah, president of Ghana, and Evelyn Evans.

grant sheet gives the "purpose or aim" as library development and the "method contemplated" as the continuation of lending services to forty districts, the inauguration of postal service to individual borrowers living in remote and sparsely populated districts, and the development of service for children and young people.[44] This brought the total of Carnegie grants to $40,000. This was listed euphemistically in a 1963 Carnegie Corporation publication as "Government of Kenya: public library development, 1930-35."[45]

In 1959 D.A.R. Kemp, then librarian of the Royal Technical College, Nairobi (later the University of Nairobi), published an article on libraries in Kenya in a British journal. Kemp mentioned how curious ideas had arisen, the most widespread and inaccurate being that Kenya had similarities to South Africa. He said that services were shared by all races, that there were no black- or white-only organizations of a public nature, and that this had been of great assistance in the setting up and use of library services. He mentioned the McMillan/Carnegie service, "at first open only to Europeans." He mentioned how in his own library from the beginning local juniors—both black and white—had been trained side by side on the same salary scales and service conditions, and how this should be noted by those who denied the existence of "something quite normal" to us. He wrote of what had been achieved since 1950, of how much more should be done, of how it could be done, "if the local and English publics will abandon their game of politics and settle down to the development of this lovely and heart-breaking country with courage and faith in the job."[46] Kemp had come from Britain to succeed Barton-Eckett as chief librarian of the McMillan/Carnegie scheme and moved to the Royal Technical College in 1954. During his time at the McMillan a promotional leaflet had been printed headed "plain facts about one of your possessions." The leaflet described the McMillan as "the Library serving Europeans all over East Africa." The twenty-five shillings a year subscription was equal to the weekly cost of seven cigarettes, of two buttons

---

[44] "Kenya Colony: Library Development," [19 November 1935].

[45] Florence Anderson, *Library Program 1911-1961* (New York: Carnegie Corporation of New York, 1963), 99.

[46] D.A.R. Kemp, "A View of Kenya Libraries," *The Librarian and Book World* 48 (1959): 157-62.

for a dress, or of the stamp for an airmail card. Other countries from Australia to Peru were struggling to establish a nation-wide library service. In Kenya the spade work had been done: "You have but to maintain what is already yours."[47]

The report to the Durham Education Committee's Libraries Sub-Committee of Barton-Eckett's resignation in 1931 referred to his appointment as "Librarian to the State Library of British Kenya."[48] This was a misnomer but also, unwittingly, a good sum up of what was to be the McMillan Library's role from 1931 to 1958. As Diana Rosenberg points out, "Public libraries are a part of the ideological apparatus of the state."[49]

In 1958 the McMillan Library stopped operating on a racially exclusive basis. In 1962 Nairobi City Council acceded to its request to take it over. Country services ceased in 1963,[50] but the service within the city was extended during the 1960s through the opening of two branch libraries with financial help from the British Council. The library service is now part of the Department of Social Services and Housing of the Nairobi City Commission.[51]

The director of Book Aid International visited Kenya and the McMillan in 1991, and while "impressed by the library and the large number of readers, . . . could see a great need for new materials." Book Aid offered Nairobi City Commission Library Services up to four thousand books.[52] The chief librarian came in person to London to select them.

---

[47] The leaflet is undated, but as it states that reserve funds have met the library's losses for twenty-one years it must have been printed in 1952 or 1953.

[48] D.J. Butler, Durham Record Office, to the author, 9 August 1993.

[49] Rosenberg, "The Colonial State," ii.

[50] Rosenberg, "The Colonial State," 154-55.

[51] . . . , chief librarian, McMillan Library, "Nairobi City Commission Library Services," undated typescript.

[52] Sara Harrity, director, BAI, to . . . McMillan Memorial Library, 1 October 1991, Kenya—Completed Special Requests file, BAI.

Chapter 4

The Lagos Library

The racially exclusive policy of the Kenya (Carnegie) Circulating Libraries was due to the nature of white settler society in Kenya, which the East Africa Women's League exemplified. The different policy of the Lagos Library can be attributed to the absence of white settlers in Nigeria and to the influence of a white colonial administrator, Alan Burns, even though he felt in 1929 that white racial prejudice would make a library open to both races an impossibility. Burns was born in the West Indies, the son and grandson of colonial administrators, and joined the service himself at the age of seventeen. He served in Nigeria from 1912 to 1924, then went to the Bahamas as colonial secretary. He returned to Nigeria as deputy chief secretary in 1929 and found himself acting as chief secretary for most of the following five years. He came to realize that the members of the Europeanized African elite were the natural allies of Europeans in Africa, and he strove to bring them into the ruling circles as much as possible. In this and other matters he was ahead of his time, and an obituary notice was to rank him as one of the greatest of the colonial service's modern governors.[1]

Burns was always interested in books, and in his memoirs he mentions how, during his first years in Lagos, he had been conscious of the need for a library but failed to persuade the governor that this was a matter deserving government support.[2] When he knew he was to return to the colony he got a brother in Britain, C. Delisle Burns, to contact the Carnegie Corporation of New York on his behalf. This letter inquired about possible Carnegie support for a library for "educated Africans and also

---

[1] "Sir Alan Burns: A Tribute," *West Africa*, 20 October 1980, 2065-67.

[2] Sir Alan Burns, *Colonial Civil Servant* (London: Allen & Unwin, 1949), 105.

the European Community in Nigeria."[3]   Dr. F.P. Keppel, the
Carnegie president, then contacted Alan Burns directly, and
Burns replied from Lagos on 7 May 1929.[4] He said that the need
for a library was so obvious that he was convinced that the
government would have met it long ago had it not been for the
difficulties that were always present, when there was a mixed
population. He pointed out that he was not writing officially
(though he wrote his letter on government stationery), or with
the knowledge of the government, and that he was being very
frank.

Burns wanted books for his fellow whites but also for the
"small but pathetically eager number of negroes who wish to
read." He knew that Carnegie-assisted libraries were free but
asked that Lagos be an exception: "The whites would gladly
pay and the negroes should be made to pay, if even a trifle, as
they will not value what they get for nothing." He was fully
aware of white racial prejudice and asked the Corporation to
support two libraries—one for each race—because if there were
only one, and it was open to blacks and whites, he was afraid
that neither would patronize it, "the whites because they
would not allow their wives to read in the library side by side
with black men or borrow books which had been borrowed and
kept in native houses, and the blacks because the whites did not
use the library. These reasons may seem ridiculous, and I am not
attempting to condone them, but it would be folly to ignore their
existence or to think that centuries of prejudice could be
overcome with ease."

He suggested that setting up two libraries would not be
"really so ridiculous as it sounds," because the Europeans lived
in the government reservation area, three or four miles distant
from the Africans. A building could be erected in the reservation
for about eighteen hundred pounds, a room equipped in the
Glover Memorial Hall in the town for about two hundred.
Another thousand pounds would be needed for books, to be
divided between the two, "not necessarily equally." He felt
sure that the government would contribute to the maintenance of

---

[3] C. Delisle Burns to the Carnegie Corporation, 19 January 1929. This and all
other letters and Lagos Library reports cited in this chapter are, unless otherwise
stated, from the file entitled Nigeria (West Africa) Support of a Program of
Library Development, CCNY archives.

[4] A.C. Burns [Alan Burns] to F.P. Keppel, 7 May 1929.

a library once started. He did not receive an answer and wrote to Keppel again. Keppel replied with apologies on 7 January 1930. In his judgement, "nothing would be lost by postponing the question of libraries for Natives till we have had a chance to observe the success of the experimental grants that have recently been voted in South Africa."[5] Here the matter rested until the summer of 1931, when both men happened to be in London at the same time and met for a discussion. Their meeting was fruitful. When Burns returned to Nigeria he spoke to the governor, Sir Donald Cameron, who was sympathetic. He ascertained that it would be possible to rent a suitable building from the government and got together a preliminary committee; its members included the chief justice, the director of medical services, and the director of education. He wrote to tell Keppel this on 18 January 1932.[6] No mention is made in the letter of separate libraries for blacks and whites; that possibility had obviously been abandoned at some point since 1929. Keppel congratulated Burns on the composition of his committee and assured him that he could count on the Corporation paying for two thousand five hundred volumes and the cost of putting up the shelves.[7] On 24 May he cabled "Corporation votes six thousand dollars library development Nigeria."[8] The proposal sheet that the trustees considered at their meeting gave the purpose of the grant as the "establishment of library for both Whites and Natives in Lagos." The project was described as "the first promising opportunity for Corporation activity in West Africa" and Alan Burns, as "the highest type of British Civil Servant."[9]

The Library

The grant was equivalent to £1,651. Burns sent off a letter of thanks immediately. A committee was set up and the secretary wrote to the Corporation to say that the library which it had made possible would be of "the greatest benefit to the African and European communities." The original six members of the

5 Keppel to Burns, 7 January 1930.

6 Burns to Keppel, 18 January 1932.

7 Keppel to Burns, 2 March 1932.

8 Keppel to Burns, 24 May 1932.

9 "Lagos, Nigeria, Library Development," [1932].

committee included the director of education, Burns, and one Nigerian, Henry Carr, the former resident (chief colonial administrator) of Lagos. The three trustees of the library property were Burns, another European, and a Nigerian lawyer, Sir Kitoyi Ajasa, all members of the colony's legislative council.[10] Ground floor rooms in Moloney Street were rented from the government for forty-eight pounds per annum. Staff were engaged to hold the positions of librarian and messenger, and the library opened for the use of members on 29 September 1932.[11]

By 31 December 1932 the library had 2,954 volumes. This included books donated by individuals and the stock of the book club that Burns had run before the library was set up. By the end of 1933 the number had risen to 4,829, by 1934 to 5,766, by 1935 to 6,785. The number of books lent during the first three months of existence was 3,484. The library lent 23,691 volumes in 1933, 30,116 in 1934, 35,751 in 1935. In addition, some books were supplied to the little sublibraries that were set up in towns in various parts of the country: 535 in 1933, 1,800 in 1934, 1,200 in 1935. Fiction comprised approximately half of the stock, and the proportion of fiction to nonfiction borrowed was about two to one. Initial classification was F for fiction, H for history, biography and travel, P for poetry and drama, M for miscellaneous, and R for reference. As the collection grew, more specific classification became necessary. This was done in 1935: M for the 1914-18 war, N for Nigeria, and so on. Burns, in his memoirs, admits that the arrangement would have shocked a professional librarian, "but at least we could find the books we wanted, and in those days West Africa had not yet been invaded by the swarm of experts who later infested it, and spent much of their time criticising the work of those who had, of necessity, to make bricks without much straw."[12] Much of the work was done by expatriate wives on a voluntary basis.

---

[10] G.I. Jones to the president of the Carnegie Corporation, 3 August 1932.

[11] This and the information that follows are taken from "The Lagos Library: Report for the Period Ending 31st December 1932" (1933). ". . . Report for the Year Ending 31st December 1933" (1934), ". . . Report for the Year Ending the 31st of December, 1934" (1935), and ". . . Report for the Year Ending 31st December, 1935" (1936).

[12] Burns, *Colonial Civil Servant*, 106.

The Library Members

In his initial letter to the Carnegie Corporation in 1929 Burns put the population of Lagos as nearly fifteen hundred whites and over one hundred thousand blacks. There were also some three thousand whites in other parts of Nigeria. Only a small proportion of the Nigerian population of Lagos would have been sufficiently literate in English to make use of the library. The cost of joining, as *West Africa* pointed out, put membership beyond the reach of most of these.[13] An entrance fee of one pound and a subscription of two shillings and sixpence a month, while resident in Lagos, was more than the "trifle" that Burns had suggested three years before.[14] Furthermore, the location of the library, which within six months of opening moved from Moloney Street to "more suitable premises" in a former tennis pavilion on the grounds of Government House, must have been a psychological barrier.[15] The Lagos Library had 297 members (176 resident in the capital), of whom 24 were Africans, in 1933; 396 (180 resident), of whom 39 were Africans, in 1934; 481 (202 resident), of whom 43 were Africans, in 1935.[16] Thus, over 90 percent of the clientele was European in the first three years of the library's existence. The remainder were Africans with sufficient western education, social standing, and connections not to feel out of place in such a milieu.

Three of these were Eric Olawolu Moore, Sir Kitoyi Ajasa, and Henry Carr. Moore and Ajasa were successful lawyers.[17] Both had received part of their education in England, the latter spending more than twelve years there. Margery Perham described Ajasa as "a man with all the voice and manner of an English gentleman," adding that "he has always been a strong supporter of the government."[18] Moore's father and grandfather had been ordained ministers of the Church of England; his daughter became the first African woman to graduate from

---

13 "A New Lagos Library," *West Africa*, 29 October 1932, 1118.

14 "The Lagos Library: Report for the Period Ending 31st December 1932" (1933).

15 "The Lagos Library: Report for the Year Ending 31st December 1933" (1934).

16 Figures taken from the 1933-35 reports.

17 Omoniyi Adewoye, *The Legal Profession in Nigeria, 1865-1962* (Ikeja: Longman Nigeria, 1977), 129-31.

18 Perham, *West African Passage*, 49.

Oxford.[19] Moore and Ajasa had both been appointed by the government to the second commission of inquiry into the events of 1929, when the women of Eastern Nigeria, believing that they were about to be taxed, rioted, and police fired on a crowd killing over thirty people.

Carr had been appointed commissioner (and later renamed resident) by the governor-general, Sir Frederick Lugard. This made him the highest-ranking Nigerian in the colonial administration. He disliked Islam, polygamy, and the uneducated, and as most Lagosians fell under at least one of these headings, they disliked him also. He believed that people like himself were not "Europeanised natives but men transformed (transfigured) into Europeans," and that they ought to be allowed to go on leave to England for health reasons, just like their white colleagues. Patrick Cole, who found these comments in Carr's notebooks and other sources, sums him up as a good example of what Malcolm X termed a "house Negro."[20] Carr amassed a personal library of eighteen thousand volumes—the largest collection, private or public, in West Africa at the time[21]—and employed two boys full-time to keep it dusted.[22] He was a favorite of the British, and in his memoirs, Sir Rex Niven says he ought to have been given a knighthood. He describes him as a gentle man of great culture and vast knowledge of West African affairs, courteous enough to treat the most junior of his colleagues as he would the most senior.[23] Burns had great regard for him: "There are many Africans as clever, and perhaps as well educated, as Dr. Carr; if there were more who were his equal in integrity and strength of

---

19 Kofoworola Aina Moore, "The Story of Kofoworola Aina Moore, of the Yoruba Tribe, Nigeria," in *Ten Africans*, ed. Margery Perham, 1936, (reprint, Evanston, Ill.: Northwestern University Press, 1963), 324, 333.

20 Patrick Cole, *Modern and Traditional Elites in the Politics of Lagos* (Cambridge: Cambridge University Press, 1975), 115. Cole tells of what Carr had to endure from his great critic, Herbert Macaulay, who, amongst much else, quoted a *Nigerian Times* editorial that asked "When will Mr. Carr learn to think like a Negro?" Macaulay's likeness is on the present Nigerian one naira coin.

21 Harris, *Ibadan University Library*, 7.

22[Hanns Vischer and Margaret Wrong], "Libraries: Nigeria, Gold Coast, Sierra Leone and Gambia," [1939], p.10, West Africa—Library Development 1936-1945 file, Carnegie Corporation of New York. This document is a 1970 retype of the original that Wrong delivered in person on 31 October 1939.

23 Sir Rex Niven, *Nigerian Kaleidoscope: Memoirs of a Colonial Servant* (London and Hamden, Connecticut: C. Hurst and Archon Books, 1982), 17.

character, there would be more holding responsible posts in the Administration."[24] Lugard appreciated Carr also, praising him and Ajasa "who with great moral courage have not feared to point the true way to their countrymen."[25] A present-day Nigerian historian, E.A. Ayandele, has described them as Anglophile collaborators.[26]

Collaborators or not, Ajasa and Carr were certainly amongst the most able and successful Nigerians in the colony. Some of their European fellow library members were equally able, and a few became prolific writers. Burns wrote a history of Nigeria, which appeared in eight editions between 1929 and 1978. It concentrated on the period of British rule and stressed the benefits it brought. His other books include his memoirs, *Colonial Civil Servant* (1949), *Colour Prejudice* (1948), *History of the British West Indies* (1954) and *In Defence of Colonies* (1957).[27] G.I. Jones, the library's first secretary, is joint author of *The Ibo and Ibibio Speaking Peoples of South-Eastern Nigeria* (1950). He later wrote *The Trading States of the Oil Rivers* (1963) and *The Art of Eastern Nigeria* (1984). C.R. (later Sir Rex) Niven, co-opted to the committee in 1935 and later its chairman, wrote another history of Nigeria. He served in the country from 1921 to 1962, and one of his last tasks was to write the first draft of *My Life*, the autobiography of Sir Ahmadu Bello, premier of the northern region until his assassination in 1966.[28] Nor did Niven's interest cease with his retirement. His book on the civil war, *The War of Nigerian Unity*, appeared in 1970; his memoirs, *Nigerian Kaleidoscope*, in 1982. The contrast between Burns, Jones, Niven, and the executive of the European library scheme in Kenya is striking.

---

[24] Burns, *Colonial Civil Servant*, 108.

[25] Lugard, *The Dual Mandate*, 89.

[26] Ayandele, *The Educated Elite*, 75-77.

[27] His brothers Delisle and Emile were even more prolific, although the latter's Marxism can hardly have been to his taste. Emile Burns wrote: "In the days before the imperialists thought of 'bringing civilisation to backward countries' as the justification for bringing other peoples into subjection and seizing their territories, the usual justification advanced was that they were taking Christianity to the heathen," *Ethiopia and Italy* (New York: International Publishers, [1935?], 67. *Travelling Back: The Memoirs of Sir Walter Crocker* (South Melbourne: Macmillan Australia, 1981), 93, brought Emile Burns to my notice.

[28] Niven, *Nigerian Kaleidoscope*, 270. Niven included *My Life* amongst his publications in *Who's Who*.

Other Lagos Libraries

What other libraries did Lagos have in the 1930s? The High
Court had one as did the three elite schools: King's College,
Queen's College, and the Methodist Girls' High School.[29]
Another, the Tom Jones Library, was officially opened by the
acting governor on 23 May 1931. This was the result of a
wealthy Nigerian merchant's bequest of eight thousand pounds
for the founding of a library and public hall.[30] Membership of
the Tom Jones Community Centre cost two shillings and sixpence
plus sixpence a month towards the library—which, however,
was open free of charge to all for reference purposes according to
Rita Akaje Macaulay, whom the trustees appointed librarian.
This must have made it the least restricted library in the
capital during the 1930s. At its opening the Tom Jones Library
contained thirteen hundred volumes, selected with the help of
C.W. Wakeman, secretary of the Church Missionary Society. In
August 1932, on the advice of foreign visitors, Macaulay
contacted the Carnegie Corporation. "We children of sunny
Africa," she wrote, "realize that education is the password of
the hour and as such we are sending forth the clarion call for
your help." The letter, though incorrectly addressed, did reach
the Corporation, which in a brief reply mentioned the grant just
made and referred her to Burns.[31] The Lagos Library's report for
1933 states that fifty volumes, mainly duplicates, were
presented to the Tom Jones Library during the year.

Aftermath

The Lagos Library was a Carnegie-funded fee-charging service
for several hundred important people—most of them
expatriates—in a colony with a population of twenty million
(1931 census figure), most of whom were illiterate. What was
its significance? Clearly it provided valuable recreation for the
British administrative and professional elite, for their wives,
and for an even smaller group of Nigerians of similar

---

[29] This information is taken from the *Directory of Lagos Libraries*, ed. Elizabeth M.
Moys and C.C. Momah (Lagos: Publications, 1965), viii-x.

[30] "Nigeria Letter: The Tom Jones Memorial at Lagos," *West Africa*, 20 June 1931,
747.

[31] Rita Akaje Macaulay to the Andrew Foundation Carnegie Institute, 5 August
1932; John M. Russell to Macaulay, 13 September 1932.

background and mind—what John Ryle, with reference to the library in the English Club in Zanzibar, has termed "the well-furnished late imperial mind, circa 1935."[32] The members kept it going with their subscriptions and voluntary labor, so that the only cost to the colony was the accommodation supplied at a low rent. Despite the small number of black members, the Lagos Library was open to blacks as well as whites. "There never was any colour difficulty," Sir Rex Niven recollected, "it was simply discouraged if not actually disallowed."[33] This put the library more than twenty years ahead of the fee-charging service started with Carnegie funds in Kenya, the service that received forty thousand dollars from the Corporation in contrast to the Lagos Library's six thousand. It put it fifty years ahead of certain libraries in South Africa.

The Lagos Library was a step in the development of one colonial administrator's thinking about library provision. After Burns left Nigeria for the governorship of British Honduras (now Belize) in 1934, his Lagos experience encouraged him to start another library. A local timber magnate supplied the building, the Carnegie Corporation $17,500 for books, equipment, and furniture. This time it was a library with a museum section: after a struggle with the Treasury in London Burns obtained permission to maintain it out of British Honduras funds. A one-dollar deposit was required before a book could be borrowed, and a charge was made for new books. (E.A. Savage, the Edinburgh city librarian who advised the Corporation on the Caribbean, had no objection to a deposit provided it was not so large as to exclude "the poorer class of readers." Savage said that the educated colored people in the Caribbean were often more reactionary than the whites and that it might be necessary to concede what he called a pay section.)[34] The next stage was to start small sublibraries in the five main district towns.[35] In his memoirs Burns maintained that in addition to the "direct educational value of the books

---

[32] John Ryle, "The Lost Library of Zanzibar," *Times Literary Supplement*, 13 September 1985, 1002.

[33] Sir Rex Niven to the author, 6 September 1985.

[34] E.A. Savage to John M. Russell, 23 February 1935, British Honduras Library (The Jubilee Library) file, CCNY.

[35] Leo H. Bradley, "British Honduras, Libraries in," in *Encyclopedia of Library and Information Science*, vol. 3 (New York: Marcel Dekker, 1970), 285-86.

and museum specimens, the library was a model in a town which needed a good example of cleanliness and good order." He admitted to finding the organization of the library and museum of greater interest than his other work in British Honduras.[36] He regretted that in British colonies not enough was done to provide libraries and picture galleries, parks, and gardens: "We see that the people have their bread but too often forget to let them have some butter with it, and they certainly never get any jam."[37] In his classic study of the making of the British colonial administrator in Africa, Robert Heussler—an American—stated that he saluted the administrators' accomplishments more than their aims, varied as the latter had always been.[38] Burns accomplished a great deal.

The Library introduced the Carnegie Corporation to British West Africa, an involvement that culminated in 1959 with the Corporation's trustees voting to supply the funds to establish a library school at University College, Ibadan (now the University of Ibadan).

The Carnegie records stop with the Library's annual report for 1935, but records in Lagos dating up to the 1960s have been cited by Sunday Oladele Ishola.[39] The fee-charging Lagos Library survived up to 1975, somewhat to the chagrin of the professional librarians who began to establish libraries in Nigeria from the late 1940s onwards. John Harris mentions its 1950s location in a wing of the new national museum building, adding that the influence of its members had always enabled it to command the attention of the authorities.[40] Harold Lancour, following his 1957 visit to West Africa on behalf of the Corporation, referred to its attractive premises, up-to-date books, and very limited membership.[41] Ishola says its final

---

[36] Burns, *Colonial Civil Servant*, 150.

[37] Burns, *Colonial Civil Servant*, 151.

[38] Robert Heussler, *Yesterday's Rulers: The Making of the British Colonial Service* (Syracuse, N.Y.: Syracuse University Press, 1963), xxv.

[39] Sunday Oladele Ishola, "The Development of Public Libraries in Nigeria," Fellowship thesis, Library Association, 1976, chapter 4.

[40] John Harris, "Libraries and Librarianship in Nigeria at Mid-Century," *Nigerian Libraries* 6 (1970): 30.

[41] Harold Lancour, *Libraries in British West Africa: A Report of a Survey for the Carnegie Corporation of New York, October-November 1957* (Urbana: University of Illinois Library School, Occasional Paper no. 53, 1958), 15.

home was in three converted garages at the Federal Palace, the top hotel in Lagos.[42] The 1965 *Directory of Lagos Libraries* contains the following description: a "public subscription library," temporarily housed at the Trade Fair, Victoria Island, but in the process of obtaining permanent quarters; two hundred registered members, those in class A paying ten shillings a month and a deposit of one pound; those in class B, four shillings and a deposit of ten shillings; persons under the age of eighteen not admitted to membership unless a parent or guardian is already a member; about two hundred volumes borrowed weekly out of a stock of some seven thousand, comprising history, travel, general knowledge, and fiction classified by Dewey; a book secretary (Elizabeth Sullivan) and three clerks; a library committee elected at an annual general meeting; and a history that started with a Carnegie grant in 1932.[43]

In 1991 Book Aid International received a request for books from the Island Club, Lagos, whose more than six thousand members comprised "Professionals, Judges, Industrialists, Civil Servants, Service Chiefs, and Businessmen of repute." The Club was getting a new library, the Eleganza Library, the building of which was a donation from Alhaji Chief Rasak Okoya. The letter was part of a general appeal, and Book Aid had been suggested by the British Council in Lagos: "Your kind gesture in this regard will immensely contribute to the nurturing of many minds."[44]

---

[42] Ishola, "Public Libraries in Nigeria," 72.

[43] *Directory of Lagos Libraries*, 34-35.

[44] . . . , Island Club, to BAI, 1 August 1991, Nigeria—Completed Special Requests file, BAI.

Chapter 5

The British Council in the Gold Coast and Nigeria

The Carnegie Corporation of New York had been granting money to British Africa since 1926, but its officers were not familiar with the area and were dependent on the advice of interested white residents and foreign experts whom they asked to visit and report. They were pleased with the Lagos Library and told the Colonial Office in London that the Corporation would do more for libraries in West Africa, if a knowledgeable person would visit and make recommendations. Margaret Wrong, secretary of the International Committee on Christian Literature for Africa, and Hanns Vischer of the Colonial Office were in Africa in 1939 and wrote a report. They were of the opinion that "any general library service should be for all communities, including Europeans, and that neither the size of the European population nor their demand for further provision of books makes it possible or advisable to ask for special grants for Europeans only."[1] In April 1940, as a result of the Vischer/Wrong report, the Corporation's trustees voted to award $63,800, payment to be spread over three years and to be made to the Crown Agents for the Colonies in London.[2] Almost two-thirds of the amount was allocated for two projects: an experimental library center at Ibadan, Nigeria, to be supervised by a European librarian who would have a motor vehicle for touring and for distributing books; and a lending library for the Gold Coast to be based at Achimota College

---

[1] [Vischer and Wrong], "Libraries: Nigeria, Gold Coast, Sierra Leone and Gambia," 9.

[2] F.P. Keppel to Sir John Shuckburgh, Colonial Office, London, together with enclosure entitled "West African Library Program: Development," 23 April 1940, West Africa—Library Development 1936-1945 file, CCNY archives.

(outside Accra), whose library was already providing a lending service by mail to European and African teachers and others.

Wrong suggested that responsibility for library organization in Nigeria should be given to the former librarian of Girton, the Cambridge women's college. This was Ethel S. Fegan, then in the colony working with the British Empire Leprosy Relief Association (BELRA). Born in 1877, Fegan had read classics at Girton, then studied for the Library Association examinations while working as a teacher. She became librarian of Cheltenham Ladies' College in 1908 and devised the Cheltenham Classification for schools. In 1918 Fegan returned to Cambridge. Many years later the distinguished literary scholar and onetime mistress of Girton, M.C. Bradbrook, recollected how, in her undergraduate days, Fegan used to fill her with awe as she presided over the library. Late one evening, as she sat reading on a stepladder, she received a thump on the back and the challenge, "Well, jackass, what are you doing here?" Bradbrook said that Fegan's wide-ranging activities—which included working in a leper colony—made her the strongest of the College's "Strong Minded Dons". Her style of dress was also memorable: "Fegs [her nickname] was the sort who wore a shirt, collar, and tie, and a tweed suit," and she doubtlessly bicycled under the midday sun in them.[3]

Girton staff who had served ten years were granted nine months' leave of absence. Fegan, who had developed an interest in anthropology, traveled to Nigeria in 1928 to conduct research on the Bachama people of Adamawa Province and to study methods of education for women and girls. From 1930 to 1935 she served as lady superintendent of education for the government. Her availability for Carnegie work was considered a piece of remarkable good luck by William Warner Bishop, librarian of the University of Michigan and advisor to the Corporation on library matters. He had known her for years and thought she was "tops" but had never quite understood what had taken her to Africa.[4, 5] The Colonial Office told the Corporation that it would be glad to engage Fegan. The West African governments

[3] M.C. Bradbrook, "Strong Minded Dons," 1993 , Girton College archives.

[4] "[Record of interview between] F.P.K. and Dr. W.W. Bishop," 11 November 1939, Dr W.W. Bishop 1935-1942 file, CCNY archives.

[5] Bishop to John M. Russell, 10 November 1939, West Africa—Library Development 1936-1945 file, CCNY archives.

concurred with the project. It was understood that she should oversee things and start by making an exploratory visit of eighteen months.[6] Her travel was delayed by wartime pressure on shipping accommodation, but she finally sailed in February 1941.

Over the twelve months that followed Fegan traveled extensively, keeping a record of the small libraries she visited, the meetings she addressed, and the teachers, administrators, traditional rulers and others with whom she held discussions. She noted that the Tom Jones Library in Lagos had had no money for acquisitions since 1934, but that the librarian, Mrs. Macaulay, had produced a good catalog. She summed up the little library in Zaria as "dismal," adding that to get in one must first locate the man with the key in the native authority treasury. She urged the oba (traditional ruler) of Benin to set an example to his people by using his local library. She spoke to the Gold Coast's director of education about sending someone overseas for training, but he seemed to think she was being "unduly urgent" as nothing could be done until after the war.[7] Librarians were needed, she wrote in her report, and they should be Africans, because they were best qualified to serve their own people. A "single temporary Training School" should be set up for three years or so.[8] She recommended cooperation between the Carnegie Library scheme and any institutes that the British Council would set up: "I have all along felt that a Library in West Africa would do far more valuable work and have more chance of support, and of permanence, if it could be combined with other cultural activities, such as lectures, classes, debates, theatricals and so on." The library could be in the same building, have its own librarian, bear the Carnegie name, and receive "supervision and advice" from the institute's director.[9]

Then the Carnegie Corporation froze the $63,800 and all other awards for projects not yet started in British dominions

---

6 Shuckburgh to Keppel, 20 February 1941, West Africa—Library Development 1936-1945 file, CCNY archives.

7 [Ethel S. Fegan], "Tour of British West Africa for the Carnegie Corporation, N.Y. 1941-2," two handwritten notebooks, unpaginated, Girton College archives.

8 [Ethel S. Fegan], "Report on Library Needs in British West Africa," 1942 , p.1, West Africa—Library Development 1936-1945 file, CCNY archives.

9 [Fegan], "Report on Library Needs," 3.

and colonies (apart from Canada), until the war would end. Referring to the West African library program, the Corporation told the Colonial Office that "it does not seem wise at this time to take further steps."[10]

The British Council Staff

The British Council stepped into the gap. Set up in the 1930s to promote a wider appreciation of Britain abroad, it extended its activities to the colonies during the war. A senior representative and two representatives for British West Africa were appointed in 1943, and Fegan and another librarian followed in March 1944.

The senior representative was W.M. Macmillan, and his appointment was applauded as really good news by one widely read weekly: "The four colonies, indeed all dependent Africans, have no more understanding friend." If Britain was less wasteful of its assets, *West Africa* went on, Macmillan would have been pressed to take up a governorship on his resignation from the University of the Witwatersrand ten years earlier.[11] Macmillan's sympathies for the African majority in South Africa had earned him the disapproval of their rulers. The citation for the honorary degree that Oxford awarded him in 1957 stated that, amidst the threats and malice of detractors, he emerged as the champion not only of culture but also of freedom and justice. Mona, his wife, cited this in the biography of her late husband that she entitled *Champion of Africa*. After his death a friend wrote in *The Times* of his lifelong concern for social justice.[12] But in the colonies from 1943 to 1945 his concern was very definitely for the European and African educated elite. He defended his policy in a radio broadcast after his return to London: "This was a case of beginning where the need is greatest—at the top. Think of those Africans, doctors, teachers, lawyers—who spend much time and money in getting a university education, how are they to keep up?"[13]

---

[10] W.A.J. to C.J. Jeffries, Colonial Office, 10 June 1942, West Africa—Library Development 1936-1945 file, CCNY archives.

[11] *West Africa*, 27 February 1943, 163.

[12] Julius Lewin, "Professor W.M. Macmillan: South African Historian," *The Times* [London], 28 October 1974, 14.

[13] Cited in Mona Macmillan, *Champion of Africa*, 181.

Macmillan set up the Council's regional headquarters in the Gold Coast in 1943. In order of precedence this colony ranked second (Nigeria came first), but it was the base for the resident minister, Lord Swinton, whose job it was to coordinate the war effort in the region. His office's views on library matters now had to be taken into consideration in addition to those of the governments of the four colonies, the Colonial Office in London, and the British Council in London and on the spot. In May 1943 the secretary of state for the colonies had informed the resident minister that the British Council was considering stepping into the place of the Carnegie Corporation with regard to library work. It was proposed that the library training school be established at Achimota College under Miss Fegan and an assistant who would later take over from her.[14]

As her assistant Fegan selected a cousin whom she had not seen in forty-five years: Kate Dorothy Ferguson, a soldier's daughter born in England in 1889 and privately educated, and a resident of the United States since before World War I. Ferguson had gone to Illinois rather than Columbia for her library education on the recommendation of her cousin, who had lectured at Illinois in 1913. In one of those grimly honest references permissible at the time, a female instructor described Ferguson as attractive "without being at all beautiful"; "a little superficial in her mental attainments" though by no means lacking in brains; and best suited for "a more popular type of work" than academic librarianship.[15] Ferguson worked in public libraries, in U.S. army libraries in Europe and in the Panama Canal Zone, and from 1922 onwards, as librarian for the Bank of Italy (later renamed the Bank of America), which had been founded in San Francisco by A.P. Giannini, an Italian immigrant. Many years later one of her successors at the bank, Marydee Ojala, described Ferguson as being very client-centered and amazingly forward-thinking for her time.[16] Her slogan was "When in need of data consult our library, or call Local

---

[14] Secretary of state, colonies, to Lord Swinton, resident minister, Achimota, 29 May 1943, BW8/2, PRO.

[15] Frances Simpson to W.J. Hamilton, Public Library Commission, Indianapolis, 28 September 1921, Ferguson, Kate Dorothy, placement file, University Archives, University of Illinois at Urbana-Champaign (UIUC).

[16] Marydee Ojala, telephone interview with author, 8 September 1993.

427."[17]   She lectured on special library administration and served as president of the San Francisco Bay Region chapter of the Special Libraries Association in 1924/25 and again in 1938/39. The assistant director of the Illinois library school summed her up in 1940 as "easily one of the most outstanding women in the special library field at this time." "You may not know," she informed the U.S. Army Ninth Corps, "but in general we tend to draw to the library field a larger proportion of the submissive, introverted type of young women than of the opposite type. When we do have women who are of the extrovert type with executive ability and the proper kind of aggressiveness, they usually are called upon for much organizing and pioneer service."[18]

Ferguson had grown disenchanted with her employers during the 1930s (her salary was reduced during the Depression) and, after the commencement of war in Europe, and especially after the death of a brother at sea, increasingly anxious to do "something more tangible than having my brains picked 8 hrs a day by the wops."[19] She was in what she termed vulgar good health: up every morning at 0530, by bus into work from her home in Marin County, back for a swim before dinner, then work for the Red Cross or target practice "so as to shoot any jap that may stray this way." But she was in her early fifties and her age was against her: the army, navy, and Red Cross turned down her applications for an overseas posting. Then salvation came in the form of a letter from her sister in England: cousin Ethel, back from West Africa, wondered if Kate would go out and organize libraries with her? "I want to do a useful job," Ferguson confessed, "an interesting one and one that will help build a better world. This job in Africa is undoubtedly as I see it—a scheme not only to educate the natives but also to counteract any of the Axis 5th column and that is what really makes it seem so worth while."[20]

Too old for an America at war, Ferguson must have been pleased to find herself one of the younger members of the

---

[17] "Bank of Italy Library," *Bankitaly Life*, January 1923, 5.

[18] Amelia Krug, assistant director, Illinois library school, to the U.S. Army Ninth Corps, 23 December 1940, Ferguson file, UIUC.

[19] Ferguson to Simpson, 16 August [1942], Ferguson file, UIUC.

[20] Ferguson to Simpson, 19 June [1942], Ferguson file, UIUC.

British team. Fegan, anxious about delays after her return from West Africa in March 1942 ("It takes a very long time for the Colonial Office to get going at the best of times"), had been telling people that, if the scheme did not get under way within two or three years, she herself would be seventy, which would be ridiculous. In the meantime she was working at the University of Cambridge Library: with the men away at the war "they have had to come down to women for help!"[21] A year later and still waiting, she was described as possessing plenty of energy by the director of the Council's Empire Division, Sir Angus Gillan.[22] Gillan himself and the director of his colonies section, H.L. Ward Price, had both retired from earlier careers: Gillan in 1939 after thirty years of colonial administration in the Sudan, Ward Price in 1936 after twenty-four years in Nigeria. W.M. Macmillan was in his late fifties. Norman Lloyd Williams and Roy Macgregor, the British Council officers posted to Nigeria and Sierra Leone, were younger men.

The Library Work and Its Beneficiaries

Fegan and Ferguson reached the Gold Coast in March 1944 and immediately set to work, the former outlining a program that alarmed Lloyd Williams in Lagos. He was nervous of the librarians' "expert knowledge" and did not share Fegan's "dream for many years" of having a union catalog in every colony. It seemed unnecessary to him to note carefully, for instance, that a library at Jimeta, near Yola, had a copy of *Britain Advances* no. 6, since the kind of books such a place would need were of the most elementary kind.[23] Ferguson reported to Illinois that a "classification battle" was raging: "I hold out for Dewey as the simplest for small collections but I am absolutely ruled out so it's either going to be the Fegan Cheltenham or the Library of Congress. What a load to add to Africa's burden."[24] "It's not our fault the two Fs quarrel,"

---

[21] Fegan to Simpson, 18 July 1942, Ferguson file, UIUC.

[22] Sir Angus Gillan to finance officer and to secretary general, British Council, 24 September 1943, BW8/2, PRO.

[23] F.N. Lloyd Williams to W.M. Macmillan, 5 May 1944, BW8/2, PRO.

[24] Ferguson to Margaret [name unclear], 29 March 1944, Ferguson file, UIUC.

Macmillan reported, "Fegan would have none else."[25]

Macmillan was concerned about the librarians' "quite unpractical ambition to be dashing round the colonies, setting up libraries here, there and everywhere." He said that Fegan was the head of the library school, Ferguson the British Council's librarian, and that should be that. The wartime shortage of books ruled out setting up libraries all over the place.[26] The establishment of the British Council Library Advisory Committee, Gold Coast, also caused disquiet. The women were unfamiliar with official protocol and had underestimated the sensitivity of the people with responsibility for policy in a colony, its government officers. What they should have done, the Colonial Office's Sir Charles Jeffries told the British Council's Sir Angus Gillan, was to consult the government first and to invite it to set up the committee: "The trouble with these good ladies is that in the absence of a definite direction they go charging off on their own and they are so interested in putting forward their own point of view that they do not take in what other people are trying to say to them."[27] The committee was reconstituted by the government as the Library Advisory Committee for the Gold Coast. In August Gillan wrote to Ferguson to tell her that the initial emphasis must be on training librarians and on organizing libraries at British Council institutes in the colonial capitals.[28]

Macmillan set out his position in a lengthy memorandum to London. He said it was providential that circumstances compelled them to begin at the "true beginning", with a center for "our select two hundred" in Accra. The Council was not a welfare organization: the education and welfare of the African masses were not its responsibility but that of the government. "Since libraries are no use to the uneducated" that left: at the top the really educated European and African doctors, judges, lawyers, teachers and administrators; in the middle the African clerks and primary school teachers; and at the bottom the semiliterate, the growing class of those who could read with difficulty. Since the third class could have few cultural

---

[25] Macmillan to Gillan, 21-22 October 1944, BW8/5, PRO.

[26] Cited in Mona Macmillan, *Champion of Africa*, 176.

[27] Sir Charles Jeffries to Gillan, 22 July 1944, BW8/2, PRO.

[28] Gillan to Ferguson, 16 August 1944, BW8/2, PRO.

aspirations it was to be left to the Education Department and the Public Relations Office. The second class was a problem, because its size might swamp the Council's modest resources. Cultural relations must begin at the top. Europeans would not patronize the Council's centers, if they were full of clerks; neither would the "fully educated African elite, who may be almost more shy and sensitive." The second or "clerk class" likewise would be "resentful of being 'lumped' with the only semi-literates—just as the 'high-brow' class is jealous of its own still higher status!" There must be no more doubts about restricted membership: "It is better so, and positively right." Here was an opportunity for the British Council to set higher standards for West Africa to aspire to; and having set them it must maintain them.[29]

Macmillan had spoken earlier about his plans for the British Council to the governor of the Gold Coast. This was Sir Alan Burns, back in West Africa since 1941. He told Gillan that Burns and he himself were of the same mind on club and library principles: "the only way to get together the races, he agreed, is first to catch the whites: who will come in, he added, knowing they will bump into a share of Africans."[30] Macmillan showed his memorandum to the governor, who asked him to make it clear that he wanted the Council to do all the library work it could and that the government would not restrict it in any way. "H.E." [His Excellency] agreed that the necessity to restrict membership was providential, he added.[31] Burns placed much importance on encouraging social contact between Europeans and Africans at the highest level and clearly saw a British Council club and library as one way of doing this.

An internal memorandum in the British Council London headquarters in January 1945 said it was obvious that Fegan and Macmillan would not see eye to eye, because he was determined to restrict activities, and given her background, she could hardly find herself in agreement.[32] At a committee meeting in Lagos in February Macmillan's restrictive policy

---

[29] Macmillan to Gillan, 7 December 1944 [1994 was typed on the document in error], BW8/2, PRO.

[30] Macmillan to Gillan, 21-22 October 1944, BW8/5, PRO.

[31] Macmillan to Gillan, 12 December 1944, BW8/2, PRO.

[32] Mrs. Ormrod to Gillan, 9 January 1945, BW8/2, PRO.

came under criticism. The cultivated elite were able to look after themselves, and it was clerks and their like who were most in need of help and most keen to avail of it. Macmillan reiterated that it was Council policy to work at the highest level: "The cultural requirements of the lower reaches must be met by local effort."[33] Lloyd Williams, the clerks' champion who had started a reading room in Lagos even before Fegan and Ferguson had arrived in West Africa, was given a scolding: "The plain fact now is that your one thousand members are being 'spoilt'—and unhappily also some of your two thousand precious books! Your present members are getting far more than their fair share." And not only were they getting the books, they were getting the "over-comfortable" chairs which were intended for the Council's own club-institute: for "untrained readers—demoralizing almost!" Macmillan was "sorry to have to be sticky," but "the Coast has to be taught, as part of its education, to recognize the existence and the rights of the high-brow!"[34, 35]

While on home leave in Britain later in 1945 Macmillan decided not to return to West Africa. This must have been a relief to a number of people. Ward Price felt that the Council should deal entirely with Africans, "that is the young educated Africans . . . the only ones which we would be able to mould nearer to our hearts desire."[36] On reading a copy of the minutes of the Lagos meeting, he commented that he was never in agreement with Macmillan's elitist policy. The Council ought to take a long-term view and not bother with European government officials who were often mere birds of passage.[37] Early in 1946 Gillan told Jeffries in the Colonial Office that most of the books in the Council's Gold Coast institute would be handed over to a municipal library. The institute itself would

33 "Minutes of Committee Convened by the Director of Education at the Instance of the Chief Secretary to Consider the Policy of the British Council in Nigeria, with Special Reference to the Provision of Libraries [Lagos, 3 February 1945]," BW8/1, PRO.

34 Macmillan to Lloyd Williams, 2 March 1945, BW8/5, PRO.

35 Mona Macmillan writes: "Certainly Macmillan was right in seeing that senior civil servants would not mix freely with their clerks, and that the reading rooms, if left to the clerks would become entirely African" (*Champion of Africa*, 182).

36 Minute by Ward Price on letter to himself and Gillan from Macmillan, 30 May 1944, BW8/5, PRO.

37 Ward Price to E.S. Bingham, Council, Accra, 30 March 1945, BW8/5, PRO.

continue on more democratic lines. Macmillan may or may not
have been right at the beginning, he went on, but the time had
come to open the door a little wider if the Council was not to be
accused of snobbery.[38]

Fegan and Ferguson also left the Gold Coast in 1945, the
former to resume her work with lepers in Zaria, the latter on
transfer to the British Council in Lagos. Fegan had prepared
fourteen students for the Elementary Examination of the British
Library Association. Ten passed, and the four who did not, went
down only in English literature, a paper she herself thought
very stiff even for English candidates.[39] They were not a bad
lot, though she was sorry to find that the two who were least
satisfactory in every way were Nigerians probably sent for
library training, because their departments wanted to get rid of
them.[40] The students had attended her lectures and engaged in
practical work under her direction and were to spend the second
year back at their posts, where they would be visited by a
trained librarian. Ferguson said that the two attached to her
were doing very good work, but she feared they would slump
like ships without rudders when she left for Nigeria.[41]

Late in 1944 Macmillan had said something to Fegan about
asking her to continue the school, but she told Ward Price that
she would not, even if the Council were to offer her five
thousand pounds per annum: "I am all for the dinner of dry herbs
and contentment herewith." However, it would be a pity to
drop it after a year, especially as enquiries, including one from
Southern Rhodesia, had been received about places for 1945/46.
What about making it into an African school of librarianship,

[38] Gillan to Jeffries, 25 January 1946, BW8/5, PRO.

[39] Fegan to Gillan, 29 October 1945, BW8/2, PRO.

[40] Fegan to Ward Price, 16 July 1945, BW8/2, PRO.

[41] Ferguson to Ward Price, 21 September 1945, BW8/2, PRO. Such expressions of
lack of confidence were common throughout the empire and not confined to
librarianship. Given Ferguson's colleague's work for the British Empire Leprosy
Relief Association, an example from the medical career of one of that association's
founders is appropriate. Sir Leonard Rogers served in India from 1894 to 1920. He
acknowledged the "great ability of Indian practitioners in passing examinations,"
but, he continued, "when it comes to practical work and I am especially thinking
of laboratory and scientific branches requiring great exactness, I have found the
very best of them unreliable in even small matters, necessitating most careful
supervision and verification of their results before they can be accepted." Cited
in Helen Joy Power, "Sir Leonard Rogers FRS (1868-1962): Tropical Medicine in
the Indian Medical Service," Ph.D thesis, University of London, 1993, 178.

she wondered?[42] This was not to be. The Library Advisory Committee for the Gold Coast decided that as the prospect of establishing more libraries was remote, it would be a mistake to enrol students for whom there was no definite prospect of employment.[43] Sixteen years were to elapse before the Gold Coast—by then Ghana—would have a library school again.

On her arrival in the leper colony Fegan found a craze for knitting among the older boys. She taught them how to turn the heel when making socks. She was good at languages, and adult patients who wanted to learn to read became her responsibility. The new Hausa newspaper, *Gaskiya Ta Fi Kwabo* [Truth Is Worth More Than a Penny] and new books provided reading matter. Later she returned to the Gold Coast, where she was a familiar sight cycling the ten miles between Achimota College and Accra.[44] She liked being in Africa and had written years earlier that "everywhere, as one gets to know the people, wherever they may be, right up-country in the bush, or down on the Coast in some of the seaport towns, one finds the same sterling good stuff . . . . Those Old Girtonians who have tried it will, I am sure, endorse my opinion that it would be difficult to find more interesting or more satisfying work."[45]

The Lagos Row

In Lagos Kate Ferguson became chief protagonist in a controversy that was to reach beyond the Council and involve both the Nigerian government and the Colonial Office. She started the Lagos Public Library, a joint venture between the Council and the Lagos Town Council. It had the stock of what had been the Council's own library and was open to all in Lagos who could and would pay the subscription of two shillings and sixpence for six months' membership. She told B. Kennedy Cooke, director of the Council's Production Division, that each colony should make its own decision as to whether a subscription should be charged or not. In Nigeria their advisors

[42] Fegan to Ward Price, 1 December 1944, BW8/2, PRO.

[43] Cited in Evelyn J.A. Evans, *The Development of Public Library Services in the Gold Coast* (London: Library Association, 1956), .

[44] E.S. Fegan, "Life in a Leper Colony in Nigeria," *Girton Review*, Easter Term 1946, 19; Obituary by Evelyn J.A. Evans, *Library Association Record* 77 (1975): 299.

[45] E.S. Fegan, "Some Africans," *Girton Review*, Michaelmas Term 1929, 14.

were emphatically in favor of a charge: "As you say, the Africans are accustomed to pay for their education, and their pleasures, and they receive a certain snobbish satisfaction in belonging to a subscription library."[46] Nigerian traditional rulers had told her that public money was needed for a better water supply, better sanitation, and more clinics, amenities that would benefit everyone by contrast with the small percentage that libraries would serve. Eventually, when more Africans would pay taxes, the public library as a tax-supported institution would come into its own; until then a small fee was the only answer.[47]

Ferguson's antagonist was Jessie Carnell, acting director of the Council's Books Department and no believer in membership fees. Born in 1906, Carnell had organized public library service in rural parts of England before going to New Zealand to do similar work in 1939. According to an obituary, she felt impelled to move on from a place whenever she realized she was happy and settled there.[48] She returned to wartime Britain and a job with the Council in 1944. Ferguson tried to reason with her as to why the Lagos Public Library must charge. Schemes had to fit in with local conditions, which was why they submitted their plans to a library committee composed of a government representative, the head of the Education Department, and prominent Africans. A membership fee was a must. The committee would not even discuss the question of reducing or abolishing it. Without a fee they would have "(a) no building big enough to hold all the riff raff that would come in; (b) how could we keep out those who could not read[?]; (c) you could not provide enough books."[49] The

---

46 She also supervised apprentice librarians and wrote to Ward Price about one incident that was too good to keep to herself. The students were cataloging a book on English country houses and she pointed out a photograph of Blenheim, home of the dukes of Marlborough and temporary home of the Books Department of the British Council. They were terribly impressed. But what could one man do with such a big house? How many wives does he have? Surely he does not live there with just one? "Our ways will always be wondrous queer to the African," she concluded, "in spite of the veneer of education he acquires." (Ferguson to Ward Price, 7 February 1946, BW8/2, PRO). One imagines that Ward Price and other recipients of such anecdotes over the years would have preferred that Ferguson had been less forthcoming.

47 Ferguson to B. Kennedy Cooke, 15 August 1946, BW8/4, PRO.

48 Mary Piggott, "Edith Jessie Carnell," *Library Association Record* 86 (1984): 319.

49 Ferguson to Director Books Department, 26 August 1946, BW8/4, PRO.

chairman of the Management Committee of the Lagos Public Library, who also happened to be the Lagos Town Clerk, backed her up with a letter to Ward Price. He stated categorically that his committee was not willing to be dictated to on the question of whether to charge or not. Without a fee the library would undoubtedly be overrun by irresponsible persons and a large number of books lost.[50] The colony's public relations officer, D.S. Fletcher, also backed Ferguson: "I shudder to think of the annual capital cost of free libraries in Nigeria to the British taxpayer which would amount to the cost of free presentation of all the books in all the libraries to such members who had been lucky enough to take them out in the first instance. In any case it is a moot point whether a large per capita increase in readers is desirable. There is quite enough mental indigestion to cope with in this country as it is."[51]

Carnell expressed her objections in a long letter to Ferguson. She described the subscription system as a hoary device that had sprung up in places, where persistent demand for reading had preceded the full development of public services. The globe was dotted with subscription libraries that had been started with good intentions but which had fallen into decay. Over and over again the system had proved to be at best a serious handicap to progress and at worst a complete failure.[52] She reiterated her position in an internal memorandum in London. She had no objection to a deposit, if this was thought an essential safeguard. But a fee! The Council was laying itself open not only to criticism but also to ridicule. What a story it would make for that section of the British press antagonistic to the Council, if it learned that an organization in receipt of three million pounds or so from the British taxpayer was collecting a penny a month from small children in Nigeria and, presumably, refusing them books, if they did not have that penny! If this was the Council's idea of fostering library service in the colonies, it would be better if it did not exist. It was in places like West Africa where wages were low that the case for free service was even stronger than in Britain. She could

---

[50] Chairman of the Management Committee of the Lagos Public Library to Ward Price, 6 September 1946, BW8/4, PRO.

[51] D.S. Fletcher to Senior Librarian, British Council, Lagos, 24 September 1946, BW8/4, PRO.

[52] Carnell to Ferguson, 10 September 1946, BW8/4, PRO.

not help suspecting that the real reason for wanting to charge was the public relations officer's fear of "mental indigestion": "In other words, we are scared of giving the Nigerians free access to the world of books." The controversy was of vital importance for the kind of work they were doing in the colonies, and she believed that her objection to charging would have the backing of progressive opinion and the almost universal approval of the library world.[53, 54]

Ferguson won. Gillan said that she had answered none of Carnell's arguments and that the public relations officer's suggestion that there were too many readers already was deplorable.[55] Ward Price said he agreed with Carnell entirely.[56] But Ferguson and her library management committee had not been idle: in Lagos the government of the colony informed the British Council that it accepted its grant of one thousand pounds a year for three years to the Lagos Public Library provided that arrangements for subscriptions were maintained; the position would be reviewed at the end of the first year.[57] In London the Colonial Office informed the Council

---

[53] Carnell to Production Division, 14 October 1946, BW8/4, PRO.

[54] Carnell's reference to the press had to do with the newspapers owned by Lord Beaverbrook. In her history of the Council Lady Donaldson describes Beaverbrook as one of the few deliberately wicked men in British history: "Others have done more harm but few have done it intentionally" (Donaldson, *The British Council*, 63). He thought culture was a waste of money, and maintained that the roar of British bombers was better propaganda than broadcasts of madrigals. The Council lived in fear of him for decades. Lloyd Williams, who was always getting into trouble, was queried by Ward Price about a report in the March 1945 issue of the *Dancing Times*: Frank Spencer, winner of the second prize in the world professional championships in Paris in 1938, had been engaged by the Council in Lagos to do a series of lecture-demonstrations on ballroom dancing. Spencer was a sergeant in the Entertainments National Service Association [ENSA], which provided entertainment for British forces at home and overseas. Ward Price saw no harm in this himself but was fearful of Beaverbrook's *Daily Express*. Lloyd Williams said that young educated Africans were particularly interested in this "art in which our country is rather surprisingly outstanding." Eighty-two people attended the first session, which was devoted to the Slow Foxtrot (Ward Price to Lloyd Williams, 27 March 1945; Lloyd Williams to Ward Price, 4 April 1945; "Report of the Nigeria Representative, March 1945," BW8/1, PRO).

[55] Minute by Gillan, 18 October 1946, on Carnell to Production Division, BW8/4, PRO.

[56] Ward Price to director, Production Division, 18 November 1946, BW8/4, PRO.

[57] H.F. Marshall for acting chief secretary to the government to acting representative, British Council, Lagos, 30 December 1946, BW8/4, PRO.

that it insisted on the Lagos Public Library's maintaining subscription fees for the time being; insufficient account had been taken of conditions prevailing in West Africa, when the reduction or abolition of fees was recommended; if thought desirable the subscription issue could be reviewed at the end of the first year.[58]

Aftermath

Due to shortage of money the Council was pulling out of library development projects in the late 1940s (although the British government was to reverse this policy in 1959). Miss J. Tomblin, the Council librarian who took up appointment in Lagos in 1948, reported that the town council representatives seemed to feel that the Council had "wished" the library on them and was now trying to evade its responsibilities by ending its financial assistance. "We are trying to give them [the people of Lagos] iced cakes before we give them bread," the town council chairman told her. Tomblin pointed out that the fee-charging Lagos Public Library was not a public library at all in the English meaning of the term.[59] In 1950 the library was taken over completely by the town council.

Ferguson had moved to Malaya as the Council's library adviser. She set out to investigate whether or not there was a reading public in the colony. There were two opinions: "One . . . contends that the Asian will not read. The other opinion, and I am glad to say that it is a much more emphatic one, asserts that he will read." Government officials, technical specialists, teachers, business and professional men, and boys and girls leaving school, all needed reading material.[60] Library facilities were needed to prepare for self-government and to instil democratic ideas in the young, some of whom might otherwise take "the wrong turning."[61] The British Council

---

[58] Miss E.K. Baker, Colonial Office, to Ward Price, 10 March 1947, BW8/4, PRO.

[59] J. Tomblin, "Report to Books Department on the British Council Library Activities in Nigeria," 26 September 1948, Nigeria: Books: General Library Reports NIG/260/20 folder, British Council Archives, London.

[60] Kate D. Ferguson, "A Survey to Ascertain the Existing Reading Material in the Federation of Malaya and the Present Provision of Books and Other Literature," 1950, 1, BW104/2, PRO.

[61] Ferguson, "Survey," 32.

representative reported on her energy and determination, and after her retirement in 1950, the head of UNESCO's Libraries Division referred to the immense amount of work she had done.[62] Ferguson participated in the UNESCO seminar on "Libraries in Adult and Fundamental Education" at Malmö, Sweden, from 24 July to 19 August 1950. Hers was the "Library Services in Under-Developed Regions" group, in which there was "almost incessant hot debate and disagreement," according to the official report, "but out of the clash of opinion came agreement."[63, 64]

In December 1945 a new Council librarian arrived in the Gold Coast. This was Evelyn J.A. Evans, who transferred to the new Gold Coast Library Board a few years later and went on to build up one of the best public library services in the developing world. Evans had a great deal of experience in Britain: inspector of branches in Coventry, then deputy librarian of York. She had also spent a year at the University of Michigan Library on an exchange. A brother serving with the YMCA in West Africa met Macmillan, who told him they needed a librarian. She wrote to the Council and said "Here I am." She recollects that she was appalled when she discovered what the Council was charging for membership in the library.[65] Her first report pointed out that a one pound deposit plus a one pound subscription was far too much when compared with the low salaries of the majority of Africans.[66]

---

[62] A. Truman Baker, "Regional Representative's Report on First Visit to Kuala Lumpur, April 1949," BW104/3, PRO; E.J. Carter, UNESCO, Paris, to J.D.A. Barnicot, director, Books Department, 26 June 1951, BW104/2, PRO.

[63] Cyril O. Houle, *Libraries in Adult and Fundamental Education* (Paris: UNESCO, 1951), 105.

[64] Kate Ferguson seems to have disappeared from view after the early 1950s, when her alumna file at the University of Illinois shows that she worked for the United States Information Service in London. Her cousin Ethel Fegan died in 1975 at the age of ninety-eight. For the last five years of her life Fegan lived in Northern Ireland with her niece and nephew, Dorothy and Richard McCreight. Dorothy McCreight never knew the cousin, nor heard much about her. She says she does not remember her ever being mentioned by her aunt (Dorothy McCreight to author, 25 July 1994).

[65] Evelyn J.A. Evans, interview with author, 20 April 1988, and subsequent conversations.

[66] Evelyn J.A. Evans, librarian for the Gold Coast, "Library Quarterly Report , October-December 1945," BW8/2, PRO.

Referring to what by 1947 had become the long-term plan to hand over the library services, the head of the Council's Empire Division, Sir Angus Gillan, felt sure that the colonies would still want advice and help: "Therefore it is safe to assume that continuity of policy, being in everyone's interest, is pretty well assured."[67] Gillan and his organization introduced the British public library—albeit a fee-charging variety—to West Africa. He was a humane man who found Macmillan's and Ferguson's elitism distasteful. But neither he nor the Council could be described as being in the forefront of the battle against illiteracy, and the libraries that were introduced were to prove unrealistic models indeed.

In 1992 the Lagos Mainland Library and the Lagos State Library Board received small numbers of books from Book Aid International through the National Library of Nigeria, which acts as a distributor.[68] In the same year Book Aid sent over forty thousand books to Ghana.[69] One of its staff, who visited the Ghana Library Board in 1991, reported that the only new books to have been added over the previous few years had come from it.[70]

---

[67] Gillan to Kennedy Cooke, 28 March 1947, BW8/7, PRO.

[68] National Library of Nigeria, Collection Development and Processing Department, National Book Gifts Distribution Centre, "Ranfurly Library Service Book Gifts: Annual Report for 1992," BAI.

[69] BAI statistics.

[70] "Margaret Gardiner's Trip to Ghana and the Gambia February 24th to March 11th, 1991," Ghana—Country Information file, BAI.

Chapter 6

Reading Matter and Libraries for East Africans

The British Council was not to have a representative in Kenya until 1947, although five years earlier it had sent someone to East and Central Africa on a twelve months' "prospecting mission."[1] This was the Reverend Malcolm Guthrie, a newly appointed language lecturer at the School of Oriental and African Studies (SOAS), London. Guthrie was a Baptist missionary who had engaged in educational and literacy work in the Belgian Congo from 1932 to 1940. SOAS wanted him to further his knowledge of Kiswahili and entered into a money-saving arrangement with the Council: it would pay his salary if the Council would pay his passage and subsistence expenses. Sir Angus Gillan described Guthrie to the Colonial Office as "eminently presentable" and "a very nice type of man."[2] The Colonial Office assured the East African governors that his approach to the problems associated with extending the Council's work in East Africa would be "realistic and discreet," and that it was unlikely that his report would err on the side of "injudicious enthusiasm."[3]

Guthrie traveled extensively between November 1942 and November 1943, wrote the report in South Africa, and sent it to London in January 1944. It ran to over sixty pages and contained plenty of forthright comment. The Europeans employed in mining in Northern Rhodesia, for example, would "want the African shown just as much of British life as they think he

---

[1] Sir Angus Gillan to Secretary-General, British Council, 19 November 1941, BW7/1, PRO.

[2] Gillan to C.J. Jeffries, Colonial Office, 28 October 1941, BW7/1, PRO.

[3] J.J. Paskin, Colonial Office, to Chief Secretary, Conference of East African Governors, 6 February 1942, BW7/1, PRO.

ought to know, in order that he may realize how immeasurably inferior he is, and how proper it is that he should remain the unskilled labourer to assist the European worker to draw wages about fifty times greater."[4] Most Africans understood "the sum total" of British culture to be the wearing of a tie and the belonging to a club.[5] Practically no East Africans had the reading habit:[6]

> This is of course largely because there is nothing to read; but it is interesting in this connection to contrast the opinion of government officers and missionaries on this subject. Most government officers who have tried to help Africans with reading matter, report that they find a real desire to read all kinds of things, and a real appreciation of the books and periodicals they are able to lend. Their judgement is that, given the opportunity, Africans will quickly develop the reading habit. On the other hand the missionary personnel with whom I happened to discuss the question were almost unanimous that the African does not want to read, and that even if he were provided with books, it is unlikely that he would make use of them.

According to Guthrie the missionaries' opinion could be discounted. They wanted people to read religious literature, and if they found that people tired of this—as they usually did —they concluded that they did not like reading. He maintained that Africans were eager to read nonreligious literature whenever they got the chance. He also said that reading would not become widespread, until cheap but efficient lighting was devised for houses. Because of "economic backwardness" only the more prosperous could afford even a hurricane lantern; therefore, British Council institutes must provide plenty of accommodation for people to sit and read.[7]

Places with a large urban population should have a grade A institute, which would have a library, a reading room, a lecture hall, offices, and toilet facilities. Those with a small urban or large rural population should have a grade B, with a combined library and reading room, another room for use as a lounge or for discussion, and an office. Small administrative and commercial centers such as district headquarters and trading posts should have a grade C reading room. These could be sent boxes of books and periodicals, the periodicals being chiefly those no longer

[4] Guthrie, "Report of an Investigation," 47.

[5] Guthrie, "Report of an Investigation," 9.

[6] Guthrie, "Report of an Investigation," 15.

[7] Guthrie, "Report of an Investigation."16.

required at the institute, "since the dating is not very important in out of the way places." A local African should be appointed part-time caretaker-librarian of each reading room.[8] Because few Africans were literate in English, the scope for Council activities would be limited to begin with, but this could be an advantage as the Council would start small and grow with the demand.[9]

He found it impossible to recommend that the Council start anything in East Africa's main city, Nairobi, because it would have to be exclusively on a racial basis. The Europeans were very well provided for by the McMillan; the Indian community had a library that seemed "to give them all that is necessary for the moment;" the Africans had nothing. The best that could be done would be to advise and assist the Municipal Native Affairs Officer, who was keen to provide something, "though it is doubtful how much it will amount to . . . . Such facilities would have to be the affair of the municipality."[10]

Guthrie was highly critical of the white settlers. He said that, in spite of being wellread and making use of the library facilities available, many of them were poor examples of British culture. Their ways of thought were un-British. They had distorted views of their own importance and exercised over the government an influence disproportionate to their numbers. They would resent giving Africans the chance to study British ways. It would not be wise to hint that social contact might develop out of Council activities. "Pronounced but irrational opposition" was to be anticipated from one corner in particular: retired British people attracted to the colony by low taxation and cheap labor.[11] One such was Donald Purves, a colleague of Gillan's in the Sudan Political Service from 1913 to 1938, now a settler at Njoro. "My advice, Angus," he wrote, is "scrap Guthrie's report and forget all about it as regards Kenya." It was disappointing and defeatist. Had the man never heard of the Dual Policy, the parallel development of the European and African races? Had Guthrie made more effort to contact settlers he would have found some anxious to do more for "the uplift of

---

8 Guthrie, "Report of an Investigation," 14-15.

9 Guthrie, "Report of an Investigation," 2.

10 Guthrie, "Report of an Investigation," 40-41.

11 Guthrie, "Report of an Investigation," 4.

the African."[12, 13] In fact Gillan was extremely pleased with the report. He congratulated Guthrie on what he called a splendid achievement, "first-rate . . . in both content and form." He told F.S. Joelson of *East Africa and Rhodesia* that the Council was anxious to follow up Guthrie's investigations in a practical manner, but that the situation was "largely governed by the availability of staff, which unfortunately often means under present circumstances non-availability."[14]

Charles Granston Richards

The impetus for the production and supply of East African reading matter came not from the British Council but through the work of an Englishman who came to Kenya in 1935 to run the Church Missionary Society (CMS) bookshop in Nairobi.[15] Charles Richards was playing tennis on the grounds of a Sussex vicarage when a missionary from East Africa who had heard of his interest in books told him about a job in Kenya. Richards had grown up in a deeply Christian home. He had experience of administrative work in the building industry and of the

---

[12] Purves to Gillan, 12 September 1946, BW7/1, PRO. Because of wartime pressure of work Guthrie's report took several months to be duplicated and distributed by the Council, but there is no explanation in the file as to why Purves's comments were not made until 1946, two years later.

[13] In 1950 Donald Purves and his wife invited their neighbor and friend, the Hon. Nellie Grant (mother of Elspeth Huxley and friend of Charles Richards, both of whom feature later in this chapter) and her house guests to a cocktail party. The guests were Mrs. Trowell, head of art at Makerere, and her African colleague Joseph (Sam) Ntiro, who were visiting schools in Kenya to discuss art instruction. Other settlers were present, and after the party Purves told Mrs. Trowell "I am so glad you brought Mr. Ntiro. The Dean of Makerere spoke at the Njoro Club recently about the educated Africans and none of us had ever met one. So when we heard you were bringing one to Mrs. Grant's, we thought we'd hold a party to meet him and see what he was like. We are all astonished. He is charming and so cultured and interesting." (Frost, *Race Against Time*, 79).

[14] Gillan to F.S. Joelson, 4 July 1944, BW7/1, P.R.O.

[15] Much of what follows is taken from the Richards papers, on deposit at SOAS, and from "No Carpet on the Floor: Recollections and Reflections on the Work of Forty Years 1935 to 1975 in the Development of Literature and Publishing," typescript, Rhodes House, Oxford. This includes sections by David McDowall Wilson, "Notes on *Tazama/Tunuulira*," and Sidney Hockey, "The Initial Establishment of Public Library Services in E. Africa." The version of "No Carpet" drawn upon is Mr. Richards' own, which contains revisions and additions. Because the work of revision is still not complete no page numbers are given.

antiquarian book business.[16] He had an aptitude for languages and commenced the study of Kiswahili on the ship to Mombasa. CMS missionaries were expected to become proficient in the language of the area in which they worked, and Richards passed the examinations in record time. He was to write a number of small books in Kiswahili on aspects of history and Christian devotion, including *Sala Zangu* [My Prayers], a pocket book for East African troops. He was also to learn some Kikuyu and Luo.

But first he was told he had to learn how to keep accounts. The secretary of the Kenya Mission had been bookshop manager and was slow to relinquish control. There was little money, the shop being "a small affair," with a stock of Bibles and portions of Scripture in English and East African languages, a small range of religious literature, educational books related to local syllabuses, a little general literature, and school stationery. Gradually his responsibilities increased, and he was able to expand the stock. Business improved, although during the war years of 1939 to 1945 much effort had to go into keeping the school system supplied with books and equipment.

Richards says that in the early years "there was not much understanding among Europeans that Africans had anything to contribute as authors." They were there to teach, the Africans to listen and learn. He accepts that he himself may have been influenced by these attitudes at first, but an address at a conference of CMS missionaries in 1937 jolted his outlook.[17] This was given by Archdeacon Owen of Kavirondo, who became one of Richards' heroes. Owen had worked in the Belfast Free Library and educated himself at night classes before becoming a missionary. In East Africa he translated a large part of the Old Testament into Luo. He championed a number of African causes, which made him "a thorn in the side of Government and a great embarrassment to the Mission."[18]

In answer to an enquiry about his work in 1971 Richards said he went to Kenya "to promote the production and distribution of

16 C.G. Richards, "Christian Mission and the Growth of Indigenous Literature in Africa and Elsewhere in the Third World: Recollections and Reflections . . . 1 October 1979," PP.MS.12/115c, Richards papers.

17 Richards, "No Carpet."

18 C.G. Richards, *Archdeacon Owen of Kavirondo: A Memoir* (Nairobi: Highway Press, 1947), and typewritten note attached, PP.MS.12/14, Richards papers.

Christian literature, with particular emphasis on stimulating local production with the aim of increasing African participation." Christian literature he defined as "the literature that the organized Church, and Christian people generally, both use and create."[19] It was to be a number of years, however, before a publishing program became possible, and he had to teach himself the trade as he went along. He started by obtaining rights from the Society for Promoting Christian Knowledge to publish locally some of the Kiswahili titles for which there was a continuous demand. Nairobi printers were familiar with newspaper, magazine, and stationery printing, not with books, and some of the first titles were "horrible productions."[20] The profits went into a publishing fund from which new titles could be produced. In 1945 these were books by missionaries and government officials, translations by various people, and books by Africans themselves, and it was "most encouraging that the last are increasing."[21] He had manuscripts in nine languages in hand. These ranged from African tales used as Christian parables by a Tanganyikan minister to a manuscript for the Kenya Natural History series by a Game Department official. The booklets in the African Home series were being translated into a number of languages. The most popular one was *Woman's Work in the Home*.[22] He published under the CMS Bookshop and Ndia Kuu/Highway Press imprints. In 1946/47 the CMS Bookshop sold 250,000 of its own publications.[23]

"Literature for Africans": The Huxley Report

In 1945 the governor of Kenya and chairman of the East African Governors Conference, Sir Philip Mitchell, invited Elspeth Huxley to report on the provision of literature for Africans in Kenya, Uganda, Tanganyika, and Zanzibar. Huxley had spent

---

[19]Richards to J.J. Hillman, Africa Secretary, CMS, London, 29 April 1971, PP.MS.12/15, Richards papers.

[20] Richards, "No Carpet."

[21] [Richards] "Books in the Service of the Church: Address to the Cathedral Committee [Nairobi], 16 April 1945, PP.MS.12/9b, Richards papers.

[22] Richards, "Books in the Service of the Church."

[23] CMS figure cited by John Ndegwa, *Printing and Publishing in Kenya: An Outline of Development* (London: Standing Conference on Library Materials on Africa [SCOLMA], 1973), 14.

much of her childhood in Kenya and was to write about those years in *Flame Trees of Thika* (1959). *White Man's Country,* her two-volume account of the settler leader, Lord Delamere, and the making of the colony, had been published in 1935. Mitchell had voiced his concern about the lack of appropriate reading material for Africans to her in 1936, when he was governor of Uganda and she was his guest at Government House. He foresaw that, "if no action was taken . . . all sorts of folk with axes to grind might step in, using cheap handprinting presses, to spread their opinions, and often lies: 'We don't want a vacuum filled with hot air'."[24] The war first delayed progress and then made it more urgent as, among other reasons, the *askaris* [East African troops] would be returning for demobilization after being exposed to a wider world.

Flying out from London, Huxley stopped off for four days in Nigeria, where she studied the work of the Gaskiya Corporation, Zaria. This was the successor to the former Literature Bureau. It was headed by Dr. Rupert East and published the newspaper *Gaskiya Ta Fi Kwabo* and other items that Ethel Fegan found helpful in her literacy teaching. The colonial authorities were concerned about the independent Nigerian press, which was lively and critical. They wanted to build up a tradition of "clean journalism."[25] There was the same fear of the power of the press in East Africa, where some newspapers were owned and produced by Europeans, and others by Africans, with or without Asian help. Huxley summed up the situation as follows:[26]

> Nothing can poison relations between European and African, and between governors and governed, so pervasively and quickly as a disaffected and irresponsible press. In Nigeria, for instance, a well-developed African press has persistently misrepresented the Government's policy and attacked British good faith, with little regard for the facts, until an admittedly difficult and explosive political situation (exemplified by the recent general strike) has arisen. The mistake, now admitted, was that no serious effort was made in time to get established a reliable disinterested press which would at least place the facts before the African public. Fortunately that mistake has

---

24 Elspeth Huxley, *Out in the Midday Sun: My Kenya* (London: Chatto and Windus, 1985), 87.

25 R.M. East, "Memorandum on Vernacular Literature in the Northern Provinces of Nigeria" (1943), par. 32, cited in Abba Aliyu Sani, "Dr. Rupert M. East and the Beginnings of *Gaskiya Ta Fi Kwabo,*" *Savanna* 12 (1991): 17.

26 Elspeth Huxley, "Literature for Africans: Report" (1946), par. 21.

been to some extent avoided in East Africa with the founding of *Baraza,*
Matalisi and *Mambo Leo.*

Baraza was published weekly by the *East African Standard;*
Matalisi, weekly by the *Uganda Herald; Mambo Leo,* monthly
by the Tanganyika Information Office. Huxley went on to say
that it would be a mistake to be complacent. The native press
could well develop along the same lines as in Nigeria. Its
influence was already greater than that of the "unofficial"
European newspapers. These, indeed, criticized the government
often enough, and such criticisms could well be misinterpreted
by Africans and exploited by their leaders. The situation could
be best treated by seeing that "the truth—objectively and
forcibly stated—is made available to the people on the widest
possible scale."[27]

Although the political aspect was to her mind the most
urgent, welfare was also important. A periodical with articles
on such topics as baby care and crop rotation would be very
valuable. It could encourage contributions from readers, which
would help them to develop powers of self-expression.
"Properly handled, it attracts readers, it builds up a faithful
following, it broadens the mind and, above all, it enables the
message to be repeated continuously until it sinks in."[28]

Turning to books, she said the predominant need was for titles
in Kiswahili and the other main East African languages. The
existing supply, however, was by no means negligible and would
be greatly increased, when the wartime shortages of printing
materials eased. The CMS Bookshop, Nairobi, had over a
hundred manuscripts ready for press. The missionary societies
were the biggest publishers and distributors. CMS Nairobi had
published nearly all the titles in existence in Kikuyu, Kamba,
Luo, and Abaluhya, others in Kiswahili and English, and
started the People of Kenya and the Natural History of Kenya
series.[29] From Britain, Oxford University Press (OUP),
Longmans Green and Nelson had plans to extend their East
African activities as soon as the printing situation improved.
The British publishers and the missionary societies could be
relied upon to meet the demand for books in English but would,

[27] Huxley, "Literature for Africans," par. 21.

[28] Huxley, "Literature for Africans," par. 22.

[29] Huxley, "Literature for Africans," par. 23.

"no doubt, welcome informed advice and guidance, and a careful watch should be kept to see that English books satisfy tastes and at the same time provide food which will nourish the mind as well as please the palate of the reader."[30]

Where literature was concerned, the first wish of the African was to learn to read and write. This meant that the greatest demand for years to come would be for basic grammars and readers in the main languages. Next came the desire to learn how to better his life and to make money: manuals on farming, bookkeeping, mechanics, and building. Then came the wish to read about himself and his surroundings: "This shades imperceptibly into politics." Simple economics was much read. Reading about other parts of Africa and about famous Africans and people of African descent such as Booker T. Washington followed. Fiction hardly featured: "There seems to be a widespread feeling that stories are for children and that a grown man is concerned with useful facts." Few women and girls could read, and those that could appeared to confine themselves to books on domestic improvement and child welfare.[31]

For Africans who could read English, books on political topics such as African freedom, Africans and British rule, African citizenship, and color conflict, were nearly always the first choice. According to the English-speaking clerk at the library at Pumwani Social Centre, Nairobi, the "intelligentsia" read nothing but politics and scorned books by local European residents on the grounds that they were always misrepresented in them: "They are fond of all literature of an extremist nature; in fact the grosser the misstatement the more likely they are to swallow it."[32] Manuals on business, commerce, economics and child welfare were also popular. As regards imaginative literature, Huxley concluded that "in the long run Africans must create their own books."[33]

Huxley recommended that an East African Literature Bureau be set up with its headquarters in Nairobi. Its main function should be "the mass production of cheap reading matter."[34] It

---

[30] Huxley, "Literature for Africans," par. 6.

[31] Huxley, "Literature for Africans," par. 29.

[32] Cited in Huxley, "Literature for Africans," par. 31.

[33] Huxley, "Literature for Africans," par. 34.

[34] Huxley, "Literature for Africans," par. 41.

should not compete with commercial or mission publishers, the whole point being "to increase the total flow of literature." It could give valuable advice to British firms wishing to expand their African markets and introduce them to promising manuscripts.[35, 36] It should have close relations with the missions, who had pioneered the production of material in African languages.[37] It should be run on commercial terms and all its publications should be sold, not given away.[38] Its libraries section would never pay, nor perhaps its vernacular textbooks, but profits from other sections such as magazines and general literature should balance this out, and it should be the aim of the Bureau to become self-supporting within five years. Profits should be ploughed back in, and the Literature Bureau should never be regarded by the governments as a revenue producer.[39]

Huxley had less to say about libraries. She recommended that the Bureau set up a central system to which existing and proposed local libraries be linked under the supervision of a trained librarian. Social welfare centers planned as part of welfare projects were making provision for reading rooms and libraries, but many were springing up independently, were poorly stocked, and needed help and guidance.[40] The libraries served should be independent units. They should receive regular consignments of books, and a vehicle would be needed at some stage to take them around. Readers should pay a small sum for each book borrowed, the money going to the local library fund with a small percentage to the central pool.[41] To provide mental stimulus, technical and professional books should be supplied to African teachers, pastors, and doctors who were posted to the bush.[42]

---

[35] Huxley, "Literature for Africans," par. 42.

[36] Huxley, "Literature for Africans," par. 55.

[37] Huxley, "Literature for Africans," par. 42.

[38] Huxley, "Literature for Africans," par. 65.

[39] Huxley, "Literature for Africans," par. 75.

[40] Huxley, "Literature for Africans," par. 68.

[41] Huxley, "Literature for Africans," par. 67.

[42] Huxley, "Literature for Africans," par. 40.

The East African Literature Bureau
and the Development of Publishing

Looking back, Charles Richards acknowledged that his publishing activities at the CMS Bookshop may not have had a great deal of impact on local people. But it was because of those activities that he was called upon to establish the Bureau through which he obtained the money, staff, and time to do what interested him most: "providing the means for African writing to grow."[43] In April 1947 he became Adviser on Literature for Africans to the East African Governors' Conference. This was an honorary post. Later in 1947 while on leave in England, Andrew Cohen, one of the senior civil servants at the Colonial Office (and a later governor of Uganda) told him that his plans were "just what the CO was looking for," and that he was sure that the money would be granted. The CMS agreed to release Richards from its service, and on 1 April 1948 he became, by invitation, a civil servant and director of the department it was his responsibility to establish, the East African Literature Bureau.[44]

The Bureau was to have five sections: general literature and African authorship, under the director; textbooks for schools and translation work, under a textbooks editor; libraries, under a librarian; magazines, under a managing editor; and publishing and distribution, under the director. Branches were established for Uganda and Tanganyika/Zanzibar. The money was provided by the Colonial Development and Welfare Fund. The Bureau was a department of the new East Africa High Commission, the successor to the Governors' Conference. The Commission took responsibility for common services such as posts and telegraphs, customs and excise, railways and harbors, and income tax.

The Eagle Press imprint was established, and by the end of 1950 sixty-five titles had been published, 350,000 volumes in all. Of these 88,000 copies had been sold.[45] Ndegwa says that the type of books published by the Bureau, especially in its

---

[43] Richards to J.J. Hillman, Africa Secretary, CMS, London, 29 April 1971, PP.MS.12/15, Richards papers.

[44] Richards, "No Carpet."

[45] East Africa High Commission. East African Literature Bureau (EALB), *Annual Report 1950* (Nairobi: Government Printer, 1951), 7.

early years, were by and large similar to those that had been published by CMS's Ndia Kuu Press, except that religious material was largely excluded.[46] There were a number of series including Africans and Their Land; *Mali*/Wealth, with books on trees, water supplies, cattle, and grass; *Lenga Uzima*/Aim at Healthy Living, with books on diet and on the avoidance of common parasitic diseases; and How Kenya Is Governed, with titles such as *The Police and the Public* and *Africans and the Law*.[47] An early publication was a Kiswahili translation of *Julius Caesar* by Julius Nyerere, later to become the first president of Tanzania.[48]

While still with the CMS Bookshop Richards had stated his belief that teaching adults to read was "a matter as important as any we have to face in the development of this Colony."[49] He took a particular interest in producing reading material for new literates. He felt that their needs could only be met as a public service, as they did not form much of a book-buying or book-reading public and in many instances lived in places where a bookshop would not be viable.[50] One hundred thousand copies of each of the Bureau's two Kiswahili books on teaching reading and writing to adults were ordered by the Tanganyikan political party, TANU, in advance of the country's independence in 1961.[51] Literacy was a requirement for becoming a party member.

Richards says that one of the things they hoped for was "not to become great publishers ourselves but to try and develop publishing as part of the life of East Africa."[52] The Bureau was in the "strange position" of only publishing, if the sales potential did not attract commercial publishers. They even guaranteed to take on unsold stock after three years as a means of giving encouragement.[53] Yet, the Bureau's publishing

---

[46] Ndegwa, *Printing and Publishing*, 16.

[47] EALB, *Annual Report 1950*, 3-4.

[48] Richards, "Interview," *African Book Publishing Record*: 163.

[49] Richards, "Books for the African Family," 1945, PP.MS.12/9a, Richards papers.

[50] Richards, "Interview," 163.

[51] EALB, *Annual Report 1959-60*, 10.

[52] Richards, "Interview," 164.

[53] Richards, "Interview," 162.

activities were self-supporting except in regard to staff.[54]
Richards regarded it as more important to get an African author
taken up by a publisher who could market his work
internationally than to publish it himself.[55] The Rockefeller
Foundation had provided a prize for the Bureau to award for a
new work by an East African. After a Makerere University
College student won, Richards put him in touch with
Heinemann. This was James Ngugi (later Ngugi wa Thiong'o).[56]

In 1952 the Bureau launched *Tazama* [Look!], a new
Kiswahili magazine. It was a cooperative venture with the
East African Standard, and the editor was David McDowall
Wilson, who also edited *Baraza*, which Huxley had referred to
in her report. The money was provided by the Colonial
Development and Welfare Fund. Initially the magazine was
not a success. It was aimed at people in the rural areas who had
completed primary education and who needed something
appropriate to read. But such people seemed reluctant to part
with their money for reading matter that was not "frankly
political." *Tazama* was bought by Europeans who thought it
would make good reading for Africans rather than by Africans
themselves. Also, distribution to rural areas other than those
directly served by the railway was proving uneconomic.[57]

The educational content was reduced and the magazine
revamped to appeal to people living in cities and towns. Short
stories appeared about African girls who became airline
hostesses and made good marriages. Budding authors were
offered the opportunity to "cut their fictional teeth" by
submitting stories themselves.[58] There were the cartoon series
Rita the girl detective, *Tazama* Doctor, and a Women's page
that touched on fashion and beauty as well as cooking and child
care. There were pin-ups. As Richards said, "people liked to
look at pictures of pretty girls—and there were plenty of them
around."[59] One of a girl on a beach covered by a large straw hat

54 EALB, *Annual Report 1960-61*, v, and other annual reports.

55 Richards, "Christian Mission and the Growth of Indigenous Literature,"
PP.MS.12/115c, Richards papers.

56 Richards, "No Carpet."

57 EALB, *Annual Report 1953*, 17; *Annual Report 1957-8*, 9.

58 David McD. Wilson, "Notes on *Tazama/Tunuulira*," in Richards, "No Carpet."

59 Richards, "Interview," 163.

and little else resulted in a Tanganyika government minister expressing his horror in public. Church circles expressed concern. Some schools forbad the magazine. But, as one reader said, "Don't take any notice of these people, *Tazama* is the brightest thing we've ever had."[60] African readership increased. A "Most Handsome Reader" competition drew 1,200 photographs, of which 550 were published. Three thousand five hundred readers voted, and there was a very clear winner.[61]

By mid-1955 sixteen thousand East Africans were buying, and many more were reading, a magazine that was neither news material "nor political in character." This, the Bureau recorded, represented a change in outlook, because "until quite recently it was customary among Africans for all forms of reading for pleasure to be decried as a waste of time and money." More than half the circulation was in Tanganyika. In Kenya the government had placed an order for three thousand copies (later reduced to one thousand) in December 1954. These were for the fifty to sixty thousand Kenyans locked up in the government's Detention and Rehabilitation Camps: the *Mau Mau* detainees.[62]

The government of the colony had declared a state of emergency in October 1952. Increasing pressure for land among the Kikuyu and the indifference of the authorities to land reform and political change had created an explosive situation. Parts of Kenya were no longer governable by the British, and the army was brought in. Atrocities were committed by both sides. Some Kenyans were caught in the middle, forced to choose. At the village of Lari, thirty miles from Nairobi, in March 1953, nearly a hundred people were killed, many of them women and children. Wilson, *Tazama's* editor, decided to use this incident to help turn public opinion against *Mau Mau*. Sidestepping government censorship, he published photographs and details of the *Mau Mau* oath. The response was "little short of sensational," and Wilson believes that *Tazama* "may well have played a small part in shortening the State of Emergency which blighted the 1950s in Kenya."[63]

---

[60] Cited in Richards, "No Carpet."

[61] EALB, *Annual Report 1955-6*, 6.

[62] EALB, *Annual Report 1954-5*, 13.

[63] Wilson, "*Tazama/Tunuulira*," in Richards, "No Carpet."

The Kikuyu had been among the biggest book buyers in Kenya, the Bureau reported, but now all that had changed. However, the government made a grant towards the cost of three mobile units to work amongst them under mission direction, and these would sell books. *The Work of an African Chief in Kenya* and other Bureau civics titles were recommended for use in the Kikuyu Rehabilitation Scheme.[64] Rehabilitation meant renouncing *Mau Mau* and committing oneself to Christianity. Detainees were only released, when loyalists in their home areas agreed. By this time the government had implemented a program of land reform in Central Province, and there was a new and politically conservative class of property owners ready to take over power as the years of colonial rule drew to a close. *Mau Mau* had lost out.[65]

The *East African Standard* had taken over complete control of *Tazama* by the end of 1955. A Luganda version, *Tunuulira*, was published in 1956, but it was less successful. Distribution proved to be a problem in Uganda.[66]

The East African Literature Bureau and the Development of Libraries

Richards was determined to have a professionally qualified librarian to run his African Library Service. Two people responded to the advertisement, and George Annesley of Westminster Public Libraries was appointed and took up the post in March 1948. After a survey he drew up a plan which made provision for a headquarters in Nairobi, a full-scale public library in the center of Nairobi and in the other capitals, static libraries with a minimum of two thousand volumes and a reading room, a book box service, and a postal service. Richards said that was "what we would like to do," and what the Colonial Office, which was paying the Bureau's costs for the first five years, might well have agreed to, but there was "not much enthusiasm locally—we were some years ahead of much

---

64 EALB, *Annual Report 1953*, 4, 6.

65 Wunyabari Maloba, "Nationalism and Decolonization, 1947-1963,"in *A Modern History of Kenya 1895-1980: in honour of B.A. Ogot*, ed. William R. Ochieng' (Nairobi: Evans Brothers [Kenya], 1989), 186-91.

66 EALB, *Annual Report 1957-8*, 9.

government thinking."[67] The governments of the territories said no. Diana Rosenberg, in her study of libraries in colonial Kenya, says that such a refusal was very much in line with contemporary thinking: "For the European, expenditure on African welfare should be limited to what was absolutely necessary and if possible the African should finance it himself."[68] A scaled-down plan, drawn up in 1949, was accepted in 1950.

This made provision for book box and postal library services and for the training of Africans. The book boxes, which contained around two hundred volumes, were for smaller townships and villages, schools and other institutions, and the stock was to be changed twice a year. As the service was "relatively small and inexpensive . . . and moreover largely exploratory," it was not possible to pay staff to look after the collections. Local arrangements had to be made, and the local librarians tended to be welfare officers, teachers, or clerks who took on the role in addition to their regular work.[69] One of the Bureau's annual reports said that as no service of this kind had been tried previously in East Africa, there was no precedent to draw on, and the possibility of failure could not be ruled out. Everyone agreed on the need for Africans to be able to borrow books, but no one knew what the actual demand was likely to be.[70]

Results varied, but the number of Bureau library centres in Kenya grew from twenty-nine at the end of 1951 to seventy-three in mid-1956. Some services had to be withdrawn, others were expanded. Much depended on the local authority or on the person on the spot. The local librarian tended to be the "weak link" in the service. Some were left unsupervised by their local authorities. Others had little interest in the work.[71] Visits were important to monitor progress. Week long training courses in elementary library management were held at the Jeanes School in Kabete between 1951 and 1955. Approximately eighty

[67] Richards, "No Carpet."

[68] Rosenberg, "The Colonial State," 140.

[69] "Outlines for Discussion Regarding the Development of the E.A. Literature Bureau Libraries Service—Kenya Section," no date [1953?], PP.MS.12/32e, Richards papers.

[70] EALB, *Annual Report 1955-6*, 2.

[71] "Outlines for Discussion," PP.MS.12/32e, Richards papers.

people benefited from this basic training.[72]

The postal service was established, because no matter how many book boxes could be introduced, large numbers of African readers or potential readers would still be outside their radius. Such people were as much entitled as "their more conveniently placed fellows" to be served. Members were required to pay a deposit of ten shillings (returnable on request if all books were returned), and catalogs were printed to help them make their selection.[73] The 1954-55 Kenya catalog listed four thousand items. By the end of 1954 the Kenya service had eleven hundred members, and almost eighteen thousand books had been issued during the year.[74] Many members who lived in the Nairobi area came to the branch to select their books in person, and while this impeded the routine work of the staff, it meant that readers got their books more quickly, and the Bureau saved on postage costs.[75]

The Bureau's Uganda and Tanganyika/Zanzibar offices had responsibility for both book box and postal services in their territories. Membership of the postal service grew rapidly in Uganda in 1955, when the new librarian, Barbara Mullane, publicized it through visits, announcements in the press, and programs on the radio. Membership and circulation figures in Tanganyika were disappointing: no more than 2,275 books were issued between May 1953 and June 1955. The Bureau surmised that this may have been due to the greater distances there, which made publicizing the service more difficult.[76]

By the mid-1950s concern was being reported. The Bureau's 1954-55 report mentioned that its library service in Kenya had nearly reached the limit of what it could do given its provision and establishment. It stated that it would be unlikely that the government would be able to increase its contribution and thus enable further expansion. The situation would shortly arise, where requests for further book box libraries or for membership of the postal library service would have to be refused.[77]

---

[72] Rosenberg, "The Colonial State," 129-30.

[73] EALB, *Annual Report 1955-6*, 3.

[74] EALB, *Annual Report 1954-5*, 6-7.

[75] EALB, *Annual Report 1956-7*, 4.

[76] EALB, *Annual Report 1954-5*, 10-11.

[77] EALB, *Annual Report 1954-5*, 8.

And arise it did. By 1957-58 the service had not only to give up hope of being able to meet growing demand, it had to take active steps to reduce the postal membership. The demand for this service increased in all the territories, and the Kenya branch was forced to turn down new applicants for a period of seven months. Then postal charges went up by 75 percent, and it became necessary to charge a ten shilling entrance fee in addition to requiring a deposit.[78] The Uganda branch reported an abrupt drop in issues, after it introduced the entrance fee in March 1958.[79] After the Kenya government turned down a request for additional money, the Kenya branch had to cut back; applications were "pouring in" all the time, but they had to be rejected. The number of books that could be borrowed by a reader at any one time was reduced from two to one, so that postage money could be saved.[80] New applications for membership were still being rejected in 1962-63.[81]

The Bureau switched its emphasis from book boxes to larger static collections in the late 1950s. A study conducted in Tanganyika and Kenya showed that larger collections that were more efficiently administered resulted in more books being borrowed.[82] It knew that practically every town in Kenya could operate a library successfully, if it were "correctly sited, properly run and had enough suitable books to attract readers." Such a service was out of the question, because the Bureau did not have the money. All it could hope to do was start with a few towns, where the local authorities would site libraries in the right places and run them properly. A few successful libraries would demonstrate what could be done.[83]

Aftermath

The East African Literature Bureau described itself as "a single integrated organization attacking problems of production and distribution" of general literature, school textbooks, books for adults on agriculture and technical subjects, and magazines.

[78] EALB, *Annual Report 1957-8*, 1, 4.

[79] EALB, *Annual Report 1958-9*, 7.

[80] EALB, *Annual Report 1959-60*, 4.

[81] EALB, *Annual Report 1962-1963*, 2.

[82] EALB, *Annual Report 1958-9*, 2.

[83] EALB, *Annual Report 1959-60*, 3.

Acting in the "several capacities of critic, literary agent, editor, financier and publisher," it gave assistance to African and European authors. It provided static libraries, book box libraries, and a postal library service.[84] However, Rosenberg points out that post-independence writers have rarely been positive in their assessment of the Bureau's library service.[85] The book boxes proved less successful than had been hoped; the postal service had to have its membership cut back; and the Nairobi and Kenya authorities could not be persuaded to provide a service open to Africans and free of charge in the center of the capital during the 1950s. Yet, it was not for want of trying, and "a library system integrated with the publishing of books, the encouragement of local authorship, the stimulation of reading and the training of staff was revolutionary rather than reactionary" in Rosenberg's opinion.[86] The combination brings to mind the book sector approach of the 1990s, where the production, supply and availability of material is studied, and recommendations are made which, if adopted, ought to result in improvements.

The ultimate aim in Kenya, according to an internal Bureau document of the early 1950s, should be "a unified public library service open and free to all the inhabitants of the Territory." The African Library Service was open to other races as well, and a glance at the premises of the United States Information Service in Nairobi would reveal people of all races sitting and reading side by side. If such a situation could exist in a library in which the books were entirely American, "and therefore of limited appeal," what would the response be to proper public libraries containing stock selected not on the grounds of publicity or propaganda, "but entirely to suit the tastes, interests and needs of all the people in the Territory"?[87]

In 1959 the British government announced that money was being made available both for short-term projects and for the long-term development of national or central library services. A library development officer was requested, and Sidney Hockey, who had considerable experience in the Caribbean, was

---

84 EALB, *Annual Report 1961-62*, v.

85 Rosenberg, "The Colonial State," 137.

86 Rosenberg, "The Colonial State," 139-40.

87 "Outlines for Discussion," PP.MS.12/32e, Richards papers.

appointed under the auspices of the British Council.[88] He reported that there were no public libraries in the accepted sense of the term in East Africa. All the existing services were limited either by the terms of reference under which they were established or by having to charge subscriptions.[89] His recommendations were drawn up in consultation with the Bureau. Tanganyika accepted them and received £22,820. Kenya and Uganda turned them down because of unwillingness to shoulder increased recurrent costs.[90]

Kenya did eventually accept library development assistance from Britain. It took over the Kenya branch of the Bureau in 1964 and established the Kenya National Library Service (KNLS) in 1965. Without Britain meeting the capital costs and without Hockey's continuing presence and persistence, Rosenberg considers it unlikely that the government of the by then independent Kenya would have established KNLS.[91] The size of its annual grant (£9,000) meant that meaningful development was impossible.[92]

The Tanganyika government, led by Julius Nyerere, was much more positive, and Tanzania (as the country became known) made the most progress in the 1960s. Yet, when Max Broome, former librarian of the North Riding of Yorkshire, arrived in Dar es Salaam as first director of library services in August 1963, he discovered that most of the Bureau's nominal collection of thirty thousand books were in an "appalling condition." This did not surprise him as the book budget had not exceeded three hundred pounds a year, and the only qualified librarian in the service had gone on extended sick leave two years previously.[93] The Bureau's library service was always run on a shoe string, and it is a credit to it that it had such an influence.

One criticism of the service that Rosenberg makes is that the number of social sciences books in the postal catalog "vastly

[88] EALB, *Annual Report 1959-60*, 1.

[89] S.W. Hockey, "Development of Library Services in East Africa: A Report Submitted to the Governments of East Africa," 1960, par. 2(1).

[90] EALB, *Annual Report 1960-61*, 2.

[91] Rosenberg, "The Colonial State," 176.

[92] Rosenberg, "The Colonial State," 175.

[93] E.M. Broome, "Books for the People: An Experiment in Library Service in Tanganyika," in *Library Work in Africa*, ed. Anna-Britta Wallenius (Uppsala: Scandinavian Institute of African Studies, 1966), 60-61.

under-represented" the use made of them.[94]   Similarly, the publishing program could be criticized for sticking to civics and "good government" and avoiding any critiques of colonial rule. *Baraza,* the magazine which Wilson edited in addition to *Tazama,* has been dismissed by a present-day Kenyan librarian, Shiraz Durrani, as a product of the colonial propaganda machine.[95] But the Bureau was a government department in British East Africa, and its director was a civil servant. Under "Politics and the Bureau" in his memoirs, Richards mentions that literary expressions of nationalism and the desire for independence did not come their way, but by the time that publishable manuscripts began to appear, the field had been developed and commercial firms could serve their authors' needs: "This was an expected (by me, anyway) outcome of our pioneer work."[96]

When Richards stepped down as director and left the service of the Bureau in 1963, he felt that he and his colleagues had carried out the task set in the Huxley report.[97] The majority of the senior staff in Nairobi were now African, and some were to hold very prominent professional positions in Kenya in the years ahead: John Ndegwa as librarian of the University of Nairobi, Ralph Opondo as librarian of the McMillan Library, Jonathan Kariara with OUP, the Jomo Kenyatta Foundation, and finally Moi University, where he headed the first department of publishing in the country. Richards joined OUP, with the brief to develop what was an office with a representative into a full branch, OUP Eastern Africa, to cover an area stretching from the Red Sea to the Zambezi. He enjoyed the work very much, and expected to continue with it, until he reached the OUP retirement age. Then the World Council of Churches asked him to direct the Christian Literature Fund.

It was not a welcome invitation. He was working for one of the largest publishers in the world, and he had kept them waiting until he was ready. His wife, Elizabeth, had her

---

[94] Rosenberg, "The Colonial State," 141.

[95] Shiraz Durrani, "Independence in Kenya and the Lost Opportunity to Build a People-Oriented Library Service," *Focus on International and Comparative Librarianship,* forthcoming.

[96] Richards, "No Carpet."

[97] Richards, "No Carpet."

teaching career in Kenya. But it was a "call back" to the work that had originally taken him to Africa, and he felt obliged to accept. OUP was not pleased. They found it difficult to understand how someone could give up such a senior position for "a post such as this." But they agreed to release him within fifteen months, and during that period he had permission to undertake a number of journeys in connection with his new work.

When he was with the Bureau, Richards had written "a few small things myself, to start off a kind of writing, but I kept out of the mainstream." One British publisher had said to him, "I don't understand you; you could be making thousands for yourself in your position."[98]

---

[98] Richards, "No Carpet."

Chapter 7

The Northern Nigeria
Regional Library

For political reasons Nigeria has divided and redivided itself into smaller internal units on a number of occasions since independence. In 1963 its three regions became four. In 1967, as civil war loomed, the regions were abolished and twelve states created. In 1976 the twelve became nineteen, in 1987 twenty-one, in 1991 thirty. This may have brought the government of a large and densely populated country closer to the people at local level, but it has also been an expensive and energy-consuming exercise. Each unit has its own governor, executive and civil service; where once there were three, there are now thirty.

In the 1950s the North was by far the largest of the three regions: 281,782 square miles (more than three times the size of England, Scotland and Wales), or almost four-fifths of the colony as a whole. Its population, according to the 1952/53 census, was almost seventeen million, or 55 percent of Nigeria's more than thirty million. The North had its traditional Koranic education, but few northerners had attended western-type schools: only 2 percent were recorded as literate in the roman script. Southerners (the people of the Western and Eastern regions) were further ahead, because of the schools the missionaries had started in the coastal areas as far back as the nineteenth century. In 1952 a Northern Regional Library Service was set up to assist with the development of the native authority (later renamed local council) reading rooms.

Diana Rosenberg has pointed out that public library services in Africa were organized on a national rather than a local basis as in Britain.[1] Nigeria with its regional and later its state public library structure was the exception to the pattern.

The Reading Rooms

These rooms had been erected by the colonial government during World War II. They contained radios, maps, and pamphlets, and their aim was to publicize the Allied war effort. The Western Region was the first to employ a qualified librarian to try to do more with them. This was Joan Parkes (later Joan Allen) who took up appointment as "traveling librarian" in 1949. In 1952 she moved to the North. In an early account of the service she compared her regional library to a county library headquarters in Britain, except that the area served and its population were much greater. She circulated boxes of books to the reading rooms and to school and training center libraries. She encouraged the native authorities to send their attendants to her for practical training. She tried to visit each of the twelve provinces at least once in eighteen months so as to give advice.[2] It was uphill work, and years later a Nigerian librarian dubbed her "Library Pioneer Queen of Nigeria."[3] In 1961, more than two years after she gave up her post as regional librarian, she gave her "decidedly sour and cynical" summing-up.[4, 5]

Allen said she had been visiting reading rooms since 1949 and found little improvement over the years. She had written two books of instruction for them, and her successor had written one, but they could have produced something the size of the *Encyclopaedia Britannica* without noticeable results. The buildings were not necessarily reserved for reading but often

[1]Diana Rosenberg, "Imposing Libraries: The Establishment of National Public Library Services in Africa, with Particular Reference to Kenya," *Third World Libraries* 4 (1993): 35.

[2]Joan Parkes, "The Regional Library Service in Northern Nigeria," *West African Libraries* 1 (1954): 7-9. (The title of this journal was changed to *WALA News* with effect from volume 2. WALA was the West African Library Association).

[3]Gbole N. Nwikina, "On the Lighter Side: Random Jottings," *Nigerian Libraries* 1 (1964): 145.

[4] Joan Allen, "Books Mean Progress: The Public Library & N.A. Reading Rooms in Northern Nigeria," *WALA News* 4 (1961): 4-10.

[5]S.B. Aje, later to become the director of the National Library of Nigeria, had given his summing-up in "Public Libraries in Western Nigeria: A General Survey," *WALA News* 2 (1956): 78-84.

used as schools, as courts, as council chambers, or town halls. Notice boards giving the hours of opening were the exception rather than the rule, and even where they existed, it by no means followed that one could gain admittance during the hours stated. The rooms nearly always contained a table on which reposed vast quantities of newspapers and journals, for nothing was ever discarded. The first books had come from Europeans about to go on leave who decided the reading room would make a better repository than the bin for what they no longer wanted. The "librarians" were either teachers who did not care for teaching, men who had been in trouble in a previous job, deserving cases who had fallen on hard times, relations of councillors, or illiterates with influential friends. They were either very young or very old. Allen preferred the former, but acknowledged that the apathy of the authorities was so discouraging that a promising young man who started with an interest in his work would be likely to loose it and lapse into idleness or look for another job.

The big problem was that the regional library could only advise and not insist. Allen recommended that it take over the reading rooms from the native authorities, starting with one province or a group of provinces, and appoint one of its own librarians as supervisor. It should also take the best attendants onto its own staff.

Service to the Region's Capital

Early in 1953 the library headquarters moved from temporary accommodation in the regional legislature to a new building in Kaduna. The staff comprised one professional librarian, three library assistants, and a messenger. The original intention was to serve the region but not the capital, but this was reversed due to what Allen described as an inundation of requests from Kaduna residents.[6] The statistics in the annual reports enable one to contrast the service to the capital with the service to the rest of Northern Nigeria. Between April 1954 and March 1955 40,138 books (84 percent of the total issued) were lent in Kaduna, while 7,437 were lent to reading rooms, schools and teacher training institutions elsewhere. The librarian was on

---

[6]Joan Allen, "Early Days in the Northern Regional Library, Kaduna," *Northern Nigeria Library Notes* no. 2 (1964/65): 73.

leave for three months and distribution outside the capital virtually stopped during her absence.[7] In 1957, 75,323 books (87 percent of the total) were lent in Kaduna, 11,143 elsewhere.[8] In 1958 the figures were respectively 101,144 (90 percent) and 11,688;[9] in 1959, 109,446 (91 percent) and 10,423.[10]

The concentration on Kaduna was furthered by the British government's decision to make available through the British Council money for the further development of a number of library systems in the colonies. This was by no means a completely disinterested gesture, connected as it was with the government's wish to encourage the flow of British publications overseas, and the apprehension of some members of parliament about what the U.S.S.R. and the People's Republic of China were distributing.[11] Nigeria was to receive priority, and the north was to get twelve thousand pounds. The British Council, Nigeria, librarian wrote an annual report that included comments on public library developments, and the report for 1960 includes the rationale behind the spending of thirty thousand pounds (including the British twelve thousand) on establishing a reference library and reading room in Kaduna. Those responsible wanted a good base from which to expand in the future, and they wanted "to influence those who will have influence": the government, including ministers and public representatives, and the many junior officers studying for examinations who would become senior officers before long.[12]

In October 1961 a second professionally staffed service point opened in Bida in Niger Province, two hundred miles from Kaduna. This was a new branch library whose opening had been delayed for years, because there was no one to take charge of it:

[7]Cited in "Northern Region, Federation of Nigeria, Regional Library Service," *WALA News* 2 (1955): 44.

[8]Northern Region of Nigeria, *Annual Report of the Regional Library Service for 1957* (Kaduna: no date), 8.

[9]Northern Region of Nigeria, *Annual Report of the Regional Library Service for 1958* (Kaduna: Ministry of Education, Regional Library Division, no date), 5.

[10]Northern Region of Nigeria, Ministry of Education, *Annual Report of the Regional Library Division 1959* (Kaduna: Government Printer, no date), 5.

[11]United Kingdom, *Parliamentary Debates (House of Commons)*, 5th series, vol. 607 (1959), columns 829-35.

[12]British Council, Nigeria, "The Annual Report of the Librarian January-December 1960" (Yaba: The Centre Library, 1961), p.3, Nigeria: Books: General Library Reports folder NIG/260/20, British Council archives, London.

not necessarily someone who was professionally qualified—the British Council, Nigeria, librarian reported to London—nor even holding the General Certificate of Education, but someone with sufficient education to be left in charge without supervision. Not many northerners had reached GCE level, and those who had could take their pick of government scholarships and training opportunities.[13] Allen had been dismayed by the same situation at a more junior level: the best reading room attendants were promoted to sanitary inspector, public enlightenment officer, or whatever; the worst stayed on.[14] When Bida finally did open, it had a stock of four thousand books including multiple copies of such Hausa, Nupe and other Nigerian language titles as were available. Issues mounted to over 900 a month in the first three months, but dropped to 550 a month in January, February, and March 1963. The service thought the reason for the drop was the limited range of Nigerian language material available in print.

From April 1962 to March 1963 Kaduna patrons borrowed 101,659 books (a drop from previous years blamed on inadequate professional supervision in the library) (83 percent of the total), Bida patrons 9,249 (8 percent), all other patrons 11,485 (9 percent).[15] For the three years April 1963 to March 1966 (the period covered by the next report) Kaduna patrons borrowed 237,279 books (a substantial drop in the annual number of issues that the report does not comment upon) (79 percent), Bida patrons 31,124 (10 percent), all other patrons 32,215 (11 percent).[16]

The number of Kaduna registered readers on 31 March 1963 was 5,616 (4,884 adults, 732 children).[17] The population of

---

[13]British Council, Nigeria, "The Annual Report of the Librarian January-December 1958" (Yaba: The Centre Library, 1959), par. 1, Nigeria: Books: General Library Reports folder NIG/260/20, British Council archives, London.

[14]Allen, "Early Days," 73.

[15]Northern Region of Nigeria, Ministry of Information, *Annual Report of the Regional Library Division, Ministry of Information 1961-1963* (Kaduna: Government Printer, 1964), 2, 5-6.

[16]Northern Nigeria, *Progress and Preparation: A Report on the Activities of the Library Division, Ministry of Information Northern Nigeria 1st April, 1963-31st March, 1966* (Kaduna: Government Printer, 1966), 4-5.

[17]Northern Region of Nigeria, Ministry of Information, *Annual Report of the Regional Library Division, Ministry of Information 1961-1963* (Kaduna: Government Printer, 1964), 6.

Northern Nigeria according to the 1963 census was 29,808,659. Thus, in 1963, a decade after it started operation, four out of every five books lent by the region's publicly funded library service went to those registered readers in Kaduna whose ratio to the region's population was 1 to 5308.

The Sharr Report

F.A. Sharr, state librarian of Western Australia, and Mrs. Sharr (also a librarian), visited Northern Nigeria from November 1962 to February 1963 under the auspices of the Special Commonwealth African Assistance Plan. Their terms of reference were to survey all existing libraries and make recommendations on how responsibility should be divided between regional government and native authority services, on the establishment of a library school, and on the best means of producing a regional bibliography. Sharr told the inaugural conference of the Nigerian Library Association that "someone of great foresight" must have advised the Northern government to commission a report: he could not recall any other country in an early stage of development seeking to coordinate its libraries so that they would advance step-by-step.[18] At the 1968 meeting of the association J.A. Faseyi described Sharr as having been "pre-eminently suited for the task."[19] He was a onetime deputy of Manchester Public Libraries who had gone on to build up a very successful service from scratch in Western Australia— another area where distances were also great—during the previous ten years. But, as Sharr pointed out in his report, he and his wife had no experience with illiterates and new literates and insufficient time to study their needs fully.[20] This must have been a drawback when making recommendations for what purported to be a public service in a region in which perhaps nine out of every ten people were illiterate. He said that the primary concern of the public library was with those

[18] F.A. Sharr, "The Development of a New Library Service," *Nigerian Libraries* 1 (1964): 8.

[19] J.A. Faseyi, "Public Library Service in the Former Northern Nigeria," *Nigerian Libraries* 4 (1968): 70.

[20] Northern Nigeria, Ministry of Information, *The Library Needs of Northern Nigeria: A Plan Prepared under the Special Commonwealth African Assistance Plan* [by F.A. Sharr] (Kaduna: Government Printer, 1963), 132-33.

whose formal education was over.[21] He clearly had England or
Australia in mind when saying this, because the vast majority
of Africans with western-style education use public libraries to
help them continue their formal education. He said that the
attempt to develop reading rooms into public libraries had
failed and should be abandoned.[22] He recommended that public
library service should be aimed at the educated, at those who
had completed seven years of education or more.[23] A model
public library should be set up in the town with the largest
educated population in each province. The regional government
should offer to supply the books and staff, if the native
authority would supply the building. In a later phase the
government should offer to supply the books for further
libraries in towns large enough to warrant them, if the native
authorities supplied the building and staff. The libraries
should not be regarded as branches of a regional service but as
independent units which the regional government was assisting.
The books, which would remain the property of the
government, would be allocated to the library on the basis of
one title per head of the educated population of the town and
surrounding district. A portion of them should be exchanged
every month or two to give wider choice.[24] As for the reading
rooms, they could be devoted to the needs of illiterates and new
literates.[25] If the educated population of a town or village
grew to the extent that a public library was justified, it should
be separate from the reading room.[26] Sharr said that his
Library Needs of Northern Nigeria, a 242-page volume, was in
line with modern library principles.[27]

Sharr was critical of the regional library's preoccupation
with Kaduna, which he described as a purely local service
primarily used by those in government or similar employment.
He recommended that the Kaduna lending service be separated
from the regional headquarters and questioned whether the

[21] *Library Needs of Northern Nigeria*, 101.

[22] *Library Needs of Northern Nigeria*, 118.

[23] *Library Needs of Northern Nigeria*, 103.

[24] *Library Needs of Northern Nigeria*, 119-20.

[25] *Library Needs of Northern Nigeria*, 6.

[26] *Library Needs of Northern Nigeria*, 136.

[27] *Library Needs of Northern Nigeria*, 2.

government should continue to bear the whole cost.[28]

Joan Allen published some comments on the Sharr report.[29] Its biggest flaw, she said, was in not recommending legislation and the setting up of a library board. Legislation might prevent the transfer of emphasis from service to the region to service to the capital. She was, however, incensed at Sharr's criticism of the use of the Bliss classification scheme—there was no reason why the North should not continue to be the only public library in the world to use it. The Dewey Decimal scheme was certainly not superior, and the labor of reclassification was not to be contemplated. Sharr had said that, as Mr. Bliss was dead and few libraries had used his classification anyway, the chances of its being kept up to date were slight. The Northern Regional Library Service had adopted Bliss in 1952, because it was used in University College Ibadan, the only library of any size in the country. Ibadan had adopted Bliss, because its librarian, John Harris, had introduced it in his previous library at the University of Otago, New Zealand.

Allen did not comment in her paper on the recommendation to restrict the public library service to educated people.

Aftermath

The regional government accepted the Sharr report in 1964, and according to Faseyi, by the end of 1965 Maiduguri, the capital of Borno Province, and Sokoto had "the nucleus of two Provincial Libraries."[30] Progress in implementing the recommendations was slowed by what a senior civil servant referred to as the failure to recruit a suitable regional librarian.[31] The service was plagued by staff shortages. Allen had submitted her resignation in 1958, when her husband was appointed to a position in Sokoto. Her deputy, Dennis Gunton, was appointed in her place but left two or three years later to join the British Council. R.L. Pearce and D.R. Spiby, two other British librarians on the staff in the early 1960s, also left for

[28] *Library Needs of Northern Nigeria*, 161-62.

[29] Joan Allen, "Summary of the Sharr Report 'The Library Needs of Northern Nigeria' with Some Comments," *Northern Nigeria Library Notes*, no. 1 (1964): 4-19.

[30] Faseyi, "Public Library Service in the Former Northern Nigeria," 71.

[31] Ahmed Joda to Dr. I. Audu, vice-chancellor, Ahmadu Bello University, 17 February 1967, Department of Library Science folder LS/VC "Vice-Chancellor General", Zaria.

British Council appointments. Miss R.A. Raddon resigned in 1964, leaving one expatriate and two nongraduate Nigerians who had recently attended the library school that the University of Ibadan (then University College, Ibadan) had started with Carnegie Corporation backing in 1960. The Sharr Report had pointed out that only one Northern Nigerian had qualified as a librarian and recommended that the region set up its own school. In 1967 the regional government asked Ahmadu Bello University, the sole university in the North, to do this.[32] There were, of course, qualified Nigerian librarians of southern origin, but these were either unwilling to work outside their home regions, or the North was less than enthusiastic about employing them.[33]

The expatriate who remained in 1964 was not up to the job in the opinion of British Council officers and others.

In 1967 the federal military government abolished the regions and set up twelve states in their place. The breakup of the North into six states meant the breakup of the Northern Regional Library Service. Buildings had to stay where they were, but books and staff were shared out. Philip Rappaport, Ford Foundation library adviser to the government of Nigeria and de facto director of the National Library, visited Kaduna early in 1968 and was depressed by the lack of patrons in the library and by the dust and weeds.[34] Dennis Gunton, back in Nigeria as British Council librarian, visited shortly afterwards and agreed with Rappaport, adding that burnt out light bulbs had not been replaced and that the staff did not seem to know what was in the director's mind.[35]

Kaduna was now the capital of North-Central State (renamed Kaduna State in 1976). With J.A. Faseyi in charge of library development it was to prove more successful than most of the other northern states in extending service outside the capital to the main towns at least, if not exactly into the "bush." By 1975 the state had six small branch libraries staffed by paraprofessionals in the six administrative area

[32] Joda to Audu, 17 February 1967, LS/VC.

[33] For more on this see Anthony Olden, "Constraints on the Development of Public Library Service in Nigeria," *Library Quarterly* 55 (1985): 413-15.

[34] Dennis Gunton to R.A. Flood, 13 March 1968, Nigeria: Books: Libraries: Public Library Development folder NIG/265/14, British Council archives, London.

[35] Gunton to Flood, 11 April 1968, NIG/265/14.

headquarters. By 1980 it had divisional libraries in Zaria and Katsina. In 1976 Faseyi said the service had written off the old reading rooms, because their administration made it impossible to convert them into public libraries.[36]

The Northern Nigeria Regional Library differed in a number of ways from the McMillan Library and the Lagos Library, and from the services that the British Council introduced to the Gold Coast and Nigeria. One of the most significant differences was that most of the financial support was provided by the government of the area rather than by foreign organizations and local subscribers. The Gold Coast Library Board under Evelyn J.A. Evans was also supported by its government. But the Northern Nigeria service resembled the McMillan, Lagos, and British Council libraries in its concentration on that tiny percentage of the population that could command attention, the literate elite of the capital.[37] Set up with the intention of serving the provinces, it quickly succumbed to the pressure for service within Kaduna itself, and what was entitled the regional library was in fact little more than the library for its capital.

Redrawing of Nigeria's internal boundaries has made the present Kaduna State smaller than its original namesake. But the need for books is still there, and the Library Board has asked Book Aid International for assistance. The Canadian Organization for Development through Education is also helping. Educational material is the first priority, because, given the high cost of books, schools and parents are "hardly coping"; many schools, especially at post-primary level, contact the Library Board, "but we are unable to meet their requests as we have no such book resources."[38]

---

[36] J.A.O. Faseyi, "Library Service in the North-Central State: The Past, Present and Future," 1976.

[37] In fairness, the British Council's W.M. Macmillan was also very concerned to serve the "lonely *educated individuals* chiefly engaged in the Battle with the Bush": that "old descriptive epithet widely applied to what is still the essential Africa." Macmillan to Sir Angus Gillan, 7 December 1944, BW8/2, PRO.

[38] . . . , Library Board of Kaduna State, to B.A.I., 6 August 1992; project proposal form; book requirements form, Nigeria—Completed Special Requests folder, BAI.

Chapter 8

The National Library of Nigeria

The fee-charging Carnegie libraries of Kenya Colony and Lagos made no bones about confining their service to the influential. The British public library in Africa purported to be for all but in reality served very few, with honorable exceptions such as the Ghana Library Board and the Eastern Nigeria Regional Library. The East African Literature Bureau made a real and atypical effort to reach out to the people. But overall the emphasis remained on service to the urban elite or the future elite. Then, in the 1960s the concept of information for development became prominent. If people in power were better-informed, the theory went, they would make better policies, and the benefits would "trickle down." The Ford Foundation's sponsorship of the National Library of Nigeria project illustrates the switch of emphasis in foreign aid from books for the elite to information for the elite. The Foundation supported the setting up of the National Library, because adequate library and information service was important for the "responsible conduct of modern government" in the new nation.[1] Ford used the words "library" and "reference," which "information" had not yet begun to replace, but the stress on the value of facts—so characteristic of America—is clear. The colonial civil servants who were the policy-makers of the 1930s had wanted the latest Somerset Maugham novel with which to relax. Their successors in post-colonial Africa wanted—or, in American opinion, ought to have wanted, because they would be the better for having—the facts. The switch in emphasis was gradual: old-fashioned, bookish Britain, for instance, continued

---

[1] "Request for Foundation-Administered Project Action" [OD-1097G], September 28, 1962. Ford Foundation Archives, PA63-01. This and the other Ford Foundation documents in this chapter are cited in the manner required by the Foundation.

to give advice and money towards setting up the British public library in Africa throughout the 1960s. Ford itself supported the setting up of a public library service in Northern Rhodesia (now Zambia) at the same time it was backing the National Library of Nigeria, though the money given to the former was little more than a quarter of the $468,000 that the latter was to receive. But foreign and international aid to Africa had begun to expand from books and libraries and librarianship to documentation and data, information systems and information sciences; the names and the techniques altered, but the beneficiaries remained largely the same.

An article on "National Libraries" in the second edition of the American Library Association's *World Encyclopedia* states that in nearly a century the profession has been unable to agree upon a definition.[2] Contrasting the national libraries of two neighboring European countries will illustrate why. The British Library was established in the early 1970s, linking Britain's foremost national reference and lending collections and the production of its current national bibliography. From its inception it has been central to the library world in Britain. The National Library of Ireland, on the other hand, was primarily a reference collection for scholarly historical research on Ireland and the Irish; until recently its custodians rarely showed interest in the Irish library world outside their nineteenth century walls. In an article on national libraries and bibliographies in Africa Hans Panofsky suggested that the most significant feature of the national library is the production of the national bibliography.[3, 4] But Nigeria had a national bibliography more than a decade before it had a national library in 1964; John Harris, librarian of University College, Ibadan (later the University of Ibadan), had started one with coverage from 1950. Indeed Carl M. White, whom Ford

---

[2] Charles A. Goodrum, "National Libraries," in *ALA World Encyclopedia of Library and Information Services*, 2nd ed., ed. Robert Wedgworth (Chicago and London: American Library Association and Adamantine Press, 1986), 580.

[3] Hans E. Panofsky, "National Libraries and Bibliographies in Africa," in *Comparative and International Librarianship*, ed. Miles M. Jackson, Jr. (Westport, Conn.: Greenwood Publishing Corporation, 1970), 230.

[4] For Panofsky and other overseas librarians specializing in Africa this may well be true, but for nonliterate African adults it is debatable. An interest in the sources of information on a country is not the same as an interest in the development of literacy and libraries in that country.

sent as library adviser to the Nigerian government, warned the government in 1963 that, unless it hurried with the national library project, there would be less justification for spending public money on it, since other libraries were already providing the services that it should provide.[5]

A Lagos Library of Congress

Frank B. Rogers, director of America's National Library of Medicine, made a three-week visit to libraries in the Lagos area in 1961 at the request of the Ford Foundation. The idea of a "Lagos 'Library of Congress'" had excited Ford's J. Donald Kingsley in 1960. He described it as something that was desperately needed.[6] A Ford memorandum written later that year states that Kingsley had agreed to rechristen the national library the federal library and to have it serve the technical and intellectual requirements of government.[7] In fact the rechristening was never carried out. It took time to find a consultant, because Ford discovered that "top-flight librarians" were very busy people who were in demand,[8] but Rogers was secured.

In his report Rogers stated that the terms of reference he had been given were vague if not ambiguous. It was unclear to him whether he was being asked to make recommendations for a national library or for improving library service to the federal government. He concluded that the latter could best be tackled in the context of the former and recommended that a national library be established in Lagos with the provision of service to the government as its first priority. Then it should serve as the national bibliographic center. It should collect everything published in Nigeria and everything about Nigeria published elsewhere. It should collect materials on Africa and on international affairs, and at a reference level material connected with national growth and development. It should not

[5] Letter to permanent secretary, Ministry of Information, from Carl M. White, May 23, 1963, p 6. Ford Foundation Archives, PA63-01.

[6] Letter to [F. Champion] Ward, from J. Donald Kingsley, April 26, 1960. Ford Foundation Archives, PA61-66.

[7] Memo to F.X.S. [Francis X. Sutton], from F. Champion Ward, June 8, 1960. Ford Foundation Archives, PA61-66.

[8] Letter to J. Donald Kingsley, from Francis X. Sutton, October 21, 1960. Ford Foundation Archives, PA61-66.

operate a public library system as the Ghana Library Board was doing—the regional structure of the Federation of Nigeria would not lend itself to this. It should do what it could to stimulate the growth of libraries of all kinds and serve as the spokesman of the government and the country on library matters. The case for a national library should be placed before the government at the highest levels, with the Ministry of Information's Library Advisory Committee taking the lead, interested members of parliament giving their support, and Ford officials helping where appropriate.[9]

Rogers made one other "principal recommendation." The United States government had offered an independence gift to Nigeria: £100,000 for books and furnishings for a library for the proposed Nigerian Institute of International Studies. Rogers suggested that the national library and the institute share a common building, or adjoining buildings, and a common book stock.[10] Nothing came of this, perhaps because the institute was a more glamorous target for foreign aid: the Federal Republic of Germany paid for its building, Britain for its lecture theater, and the United States for its library.[11]

Rogers submitted an additional three-page report on how exactly Ford might help with the establishment of a national library and what it might cost.[12] He suggested that the Foundation pay for a fifty thousand square foot library building (£185,000, which was slightly more than the cost of the Central Bank of Nigeria building); supply an adviser (who might ultimately become the director) for eighteen months (£10,000); supply eighteen months of other consultative help (£10,000); provide scholarships to the Ibadan library school (£9,000) and books towards starting off the collection (£50,000). Rogers recommended a total of £264,000 or $739,200, more than two-thirds of which would be spent on the building. (Eventually Ford was to spend $468,000 on the National Library of Nigeria,

---

[9] Frank B. Rogers, "Report of a Survey of Lagos Area Libraries of the Federal Government of Nigeria 16 February - 9 March 1961, for the Ford Foundation." Ford Foundation Archives, PA61-66 Attachment File.

[10] Rogers, "Report of a Survey."

[11] Irene Kluzek, "The Library of the Nigerian Institute of International Affairs," *Nigerian Libraries* 4 (1968): 76-77.

[12] Frank Rogers, "Possible Roles for the Ford Foundation" [Tab B], March 13, 1961. Ford Foundation Archives, PA61-66 Attachment File.

but none of that was allocated for a building, and "temporary" accommodation continued to be used in Lagos).

Rogers stressed that, if Ford decided to support the national library project, it should do so on the understanding that it was providing the initial momentum and capital only. The Nigerian government must be resolved to take over from there.

Kingsley, when forwarding the report from Lagos to New York, said it was so good that the government had canceled its request to UNESCO for help and was proceeding with its recommendations.[13] At Ford headquarters F. Champion Ward described it as "one of the most lean, sinewy, and actionable documents we've had in some time."[14] The West African Library Association at its 1961 annual general meeting received the report with warmth. Its secretary wrote to thank the Ford Foundation for "making its dreams come true."[15]

Library Advice: Carl M. White and Irving S. Lieberman

The first library adviser to the federal government was an American, Carl M. White, and as events turned out he was to have two successors, each acting as national librarian without having the title. White was a professor at Columbia University, New York, and a former dean of its library school and director of its libraries. After nearly twenty years at Columbia White left at the age of fifty-nine for an appointment as program specialist in library development with Ford. His first posting was to Nigeria for two years, and he recalled how on 1 March 1962, when he reported for duty to the Ministry of Information, he was told that not a farthing in the government's new £670 million six-year development plan had been allocated for a national library. It had been passed over as a luxury that could wait. He pushed ahead anyway, encouraged by public expressions of support from the prime minister, Sir Abubakar Tafawa Balewa, and the governor-general (later the president), Nnamdi Azikiwe, and, no doubt, by Ford and its resources. He submitted recommendations to the

---

[13] Letter to [F.] Champ[ion Ward], from [J.] Don[ald Kingsley], March 22, 1961. Ford Foundation Archives, PA61-66.

[14] Letter to J. Donald Kingsley, from F. Champion Ward, March 29, 1961. Ford Foundation Archives, PA61-66.

[15] Letter to J.D. Kingsley, from Gbole N. Nwikina, June 28, 1961. Ford Foundation Archives, PA61-66.

ministry in May, and the ministry leased temporary premises, arranged a small operating budget, and asked Ford for the aid that White had recommended it ask for. Ford allocated $168,000 with which to hire expatriate librarians and buy sets of the British Museum and Library of Congress printed catalogs and other bibliographic reference works. The National Library of Nigeria was on its way, though it did not open its doors until November 1964.

In 1964 the Ministry of Information published White's sixty-page account of progress so far.[16] He wanted, he said, to take the story to the people of Nigeria, to get the ideas of colleagues in learned institutions, business and government, and to leave something on record that might be helpful. He showed political astuteness in including an approving comment from the president and in chronicling the help given by Nigerian politicians and administrators sympathetic to the project. As one would expect, White's own views about libraries, information, knowledge, and society permeate his report. Some are striking, for example: "A man's opinion on political or other issues depends less on his political or social status than on his information, for a person's judgement is no better than the background of information on which his judgement is based."[17] He also said that "Nigeria is going to be administered in the critical years ahead by a generation of men and women who, themselves, will not benefit from obliterating illiteracy."[18]

White's concern was for those at the top. He recommended that "local use of the National Library be planned in terms of the books and information needs of Government workers and other leaders in the capital city."[19] For those at the very top such as government ministers he included a private VIP reading lounge in the specifications that he drew up for the planned new building. But White acknowledged that the national library could not be indifferent to the needs of the people on its doorstep who were not included in his select total: the workers, housewives, children, and students of Lagos. To help these he

---

16 Carl M. White, *The National Library of Nigeria: Growth of the Idea, Problems and Progress* (Lagos: Federal Ministry of Information, 1964).

17 White, *National Library of Nigeria*, 11.

18 White, *National Library of Nigeria*, 21.

19 White, *National Library of Nigeria*, 20.

supplied the town council with a consultant of "top-notch ability":[20] Irving S. Lieberman, also an American, who was director of the University of Washington library school and visiting advisory director of the University of Ibadan library school for 1963/64.

However, Lieberman showed as little interest in the predominantly nonliterate "public" as White, although unlike some other foreign librarians he did appreciate the importance of the library as a study place for students. But as to stock! Lieberman evaluated the Lagos city library collection against lists of books recommended for American and British libraries and found it sadly wanting. He did not evaluate it against lists of Nigerian and other African publications, nor of publications about Nigeria and Africa issued abroad. He contrasted the size of the collection with those of the regional library services and found it was the smallest. The estimated population of the twenty-seven square mile federal capital area was 450,000. The number of adults and children who were registered members of the two Lagos city library service points in 1962/63 was 4,216. White did not bring these figures together, which would have revealed that less than 1 percent of the "public" were library members. However, he did urge the dropping of the subscription charge that Kate Ferguson had insisted on in 1946. He acknowledged his good fortune in having the latest published British and American public library standards when preparing his survey and recommended that the Lagos city library use them for self-evaluation.[21]

Library Advice: Priscilla Taylor and Philip Rappaport

White's two years on the national library project were to end in February 1964, but David Heaps, the Ford representative in Lagos, agreed to let him stay on until the end of that year. Ford was anxious to hurry the Nigerian government into appointing a director for the library, an appointment that for various reasons was not in fact to be made until 1971. By late 1964 it was obvious that there would be delay, and Ford agreed that White should be succeeded by another adviser. Heaps believed that White

---

[20] Carl M. White, "Appendix A," in Irving Lieberman, *A Survey of the Lagos City Library* (Lagos: Lagos City Council, 1964), 89.

[21] Lieberman, *Survey*.

would have liked to stay on, but he did not feel that White should: advisers who participated in the birth of a project tended to turn into overprotective mothers.[22]

The second library adviser was A. Priscilla Taylor, a forty-one-year-old New Zealander with twenty years' experience in public library work in her home country and in New York. In 1962 she had gone to Singapore under New Zealand auspices to help set up a national library. She was suggested for Lagos by a fellow New Zealand librarian, John Harris, who had been at Ibadan since 1948. Her tenure as adviser was short, just sixteen months, because she married Harris in December 1965. Heaps quipped that the marriage was "a legal merger between the national library and the University of Ibadan."[23] A later chairman of the National Library Board wrote after her death in 1974: "Having accomplished so much for the advancement of librarianship in Nigeria, and looking ahead to make further contributions, she proceeded and married Professor Harris who had been acclaimed [as] the [country's] 'Father of Librarianship'."[24] She was a woman who was not afraid to express her mind. A few weeks after she left her job as library adviser, she went back to the premises on a visit, accompanied by her husband, and she presented her former colleagues with copies of the pocket edition of the *Oxford English Dictionary*. This still rankled in at least one Nigerian breast nearly twenty years later.[25]

Carl White had worked in such prestigious research libraries as Illinois and Columbia and in library schools. Priscilla Taylor had a public library background. But she did not veer from her predecessor's policy of service to the important. A fact sheet bearing her signature states that reference, information, and reading facilities are offered to the president, the judiciary, the council of ministers, members of the Senate and the House of Representatives; members of the boards and senior officers of statutory corporations; senior government officers; diplomatic missions; senior officers of the United Nations and other

[22] Letter to J. Donald Kingsley, from David Heaps, December 3, 1963. Ford Foundation Archives, PA63-01.

[23] Memo to J. Donald Kingsley, from David Heaps, October 22, 1965. Ford Foundation Archives, PA63-01.

[24] R.A. Adeleye, cited in *New Zealand Libraries* 37 (1974): 137.

[25] Olu. Odumosu, "Reflections on the Beginnings," *Nigerbiblios* 9 (1984): 139.

international organizations; senior members of universities and approved commercial firms; members of professional organizations and learned societies; and librarians, graduate students, and other research workers.[26]

The third library adviser was Philip Rappaport, a thirty-six-year-old American who had worked with the New York State Department of Labor since 1957. Rappaport served for five years, which was longer than anticipated because of the nonappointment of a director. When the directorship was first advertised in 1964, no suitable candidate came forward: the salaries paid by the federal government were lower than a librarian could get from other employers, and the institution was unattractive, because the 1964 National Library Act restricted its activities to the federal capital territory.[27] A suitable Nigerian was offered the post in 1966,[28] but he left Lagos for the Eastern Region, his home area, during the uncertainties that culminated in the East's attempted secession as the Republic of Biafra and the Nigerian civil war.[29] By the end of the war the deputy director, S.B. Aje, was waiting in the wings to take over.

Rappaport, the last of the advisers, continued on his predecessors' policies. He expressed the hope that the national library would become one of Africa's great research facilities.[30] In 1971 he stated that the library had become an effective tool for the planners of development programs.[31] Illiteracy was not its business. The branches that the library was planning to establish in the capital cities of each state in the country as a result of 1970 legislation were not intended as a medium for increasing literacy or for preventing the already literate from

---

[26] A. Priscilla Taylor, "National Library of Nigeria: Fact Sheet," December 9, 1965.

[27] "Minutes of the First Meeting of the National Library Board Held in the Board Room of the Federal Ministry of Information on 13th and 14th April, 1966," p.4. Ford Foundation Archives PA63-01.

[28] Attachment to letter to David Heaps, from Philip Rappaport, January 19, 1967. Ford Foundation Archives, PA63-01.

[29] Request OD-2001 to McGeorge Bundy, from David E. Bell, August 24, 1967, p.3. Ford Foundation Archives, PA63-01.

[30] National Library of Nigeria, *Annual Report 1967/68* (Lagos: National Library of Nigeria, 1969), 2.

[31] Philip Rappaport, "Libraries in Nigeria: Background Paper on the Development of Libraries in Nigeria Presented . . . to Ford Foundation Seminar March 15-17, 1971," p.10. Ford Foundation, Report 004234.

losing the skill. This function, he said, clearly belonged to the state [or "public"] libraries.[32]

Aftermath

By the mid-1970s the National Library of Nigeria had 150,000 volumes, 7,000 reels of microfilm, and 2,500 journal subscriptions. It had three hundred employees of whom over thirty were professionally trained librarians.[33] It still occupied temporary premises in Lagos, but it had started to establish branches in some of the capitals of the then nineteen states of the country. The establishment of state branches was required under the 1970 National Library Decree, making the institution unique amongst national libraries. Rappaport in 1971 had suggested that the branches should be associated with the public libraries in state capitals, perhaps occupying the second floor of the same building or a separate wing. This would save on building costs and on the cost of expensive material.[34] One could argue that some duplication would be bound to occur and that the simplest and cheapest way would have been to spend the money on extending existing services within the states rather than on introducing yet another institution.

Ford aid to the National Library of Nigeria ceased with the departure of Philip Rappaport in 1971, and the foundation closed its files on the grant in 1975. The greater part of the $468,000 had gone towards the salaries of expatriate librarians, the remainder on bibliographic reference works, books, equipment, scholarships, and travel awards. The Ford officer who visited the national library in April 1975 said that a professional librarian from the United States might consider the spending of almost half a million dollars excessive for what had been achieved, but the objectives of the grant had been fulfilled even if the cost was high. More emphasis should have been placed on scholarships and training. Would Ford do it again? Hardly, with program areas that appear more

---

[32] Philip Rappaport, "Libraries and Library Development in Nigeria: An Assessment of Present Trends and Recommendations for Future Government Involvement and Policy" (1971), pp.43-44. Ford Foundation Archives, Report 004235.

[33] Simeon B. Aje, "National Libraries in Developing Countries," in *Advances in Librarianship* no. 12 (New York: Academic Press, 1977), 129.

[34] Rappaport, "Libraries and Library Development in Nigeria," p.39.

pressing.[35] But, commented another officer, Ford did have the resources in the 1960s, and the staff who proposed the grant seem to have made a sound investment.[36]

In 1985 K.J. Mchombu argued that not all less developed countries needed "orthodox" national libraries. He pointed out that new institutions were a burden on meager resources and suggested a sharing of the national library role as an alternative.[37]

In 1992 the National Library of Nigeria received 27,870 volumes for distribution from Book Aid International.[38]

---

[35] "Final Report and Evaluation of Grant to National Library of Nigeria," [1975], pp.14-16. Ford Foundation Archives, PA63-01.

[36] Memo to David E. Bell, from David R. Smock, August 13, 1975. Ford Foundation Archives, PA63-01.

[37] K.J. Mchombu, "Alternatives to the National Library in Less Developed Countries," *Libri* 35 (1985): 227-49.

[38]National Library of Nigeria, Collection Development and Processing Department, National Book Gifts Distribution Centre, "Ranfurly Library Service Book Gifts: Annual Report for 1992," BAI files.

Chapter 9

Library Development in Africa: Issues and Questions

The 1950s and 1960s were years of excitement and promise. Colonial rule was drawing to a close, and everything seemed possible. Education was expanding rapidly, and the new institutions of higher education were charged with the responsibility of producing the men and women who would take over from the departing Europeans. Vigorous adult literacy campaigns were underway in countries such as Tanzania. Professional associations were getting off the ground, professional journals being founded. British publishers active in exporting were enthusiastic about the expanding markets for their products and were starting to signup talented Africans to write books for their lists. They based representatives in Ibadan, Nairobi, and other cities, and branch offices developed and later became independent companies.

The new libraries were full of books and readers. Visiting West Africa in 1964, the president of the Library Association, F.M. Gardner, said that the new Accra Central Library in Ghana made one realize what could be done with faith, energy, and support. As for Eastern Nigeria, any of its library buildings could be set down in England and be admired, any of its senior staff hold similar positions in England with confidence.[1] The standard of fiction in the Nigerian public libraries he visited was "a little higher than in an English branch." W. Somerset Maugham, Iris Murdoch, Graham Greene, John Masters, Compton Mackenzie, and E.M. Forster were always well represented, though Gardner would have liked to have seen "more frankly popular" material as well. There were few

---

[1] F.M. Gardner, "The President's Page," *Library Association Record* 66 (1964): 586, 587.

thrillers, westerns, or what his staff in England referred to as "light love." It did seem to him, however, that "too many trained librarians were concerned with the mechanics of providing the library and its services, and not enough with its actual and potential use."[2]

Two papers at a conference held in Norrköping, Sweden, on 30-31 August 1965 illustrate both the achievements and the challenges of library development at the time. Evelyn J.A. Evans, director of the Ghana Library Board, spoke of the work of twenty years. She said that Ghana had done it all (or virtually all) itself, and that its success was largely due to government support. Such support was crucial, because it was recurrent expenditure that was likely to prove a problem, not the initial expense of setting up a project.[3] Evans was to step down as director in December 1965. Kwame Nkrumah, who as president had given his support, was to be overthrown while out of the country on a state visit in February 1966.

In East Africa the new Tanzania Library Service was developing rapidly. Max Broome, who had taken up appointment as director in August 1963, said that competitive tenders to build six branch libraries—to be paid for out of a development loan from Britain—were about to be invited. Because of the large size of the country and its poor roads, mobile services would have to wait until later, when static libraries out of which they could operate would be in place. Phase one of the new Central Library in Dar es Salaam was about to be built with assistance from the British Council.[4] Capital costs aside, a recurring budget of almost £60,000 was provided by the Ministry of Education and by local authorities, who were "eager to make sacrifices" in order to secure libraries.[5] The number of professional librarians had risen from one (Broome himself) to twelve within two years. There was much to do, and corners would have to be cut where necessary to ensure rapid development.[6]

---

2 F.M. Gardner, "The Final Page," *Library Association Record* 67 (1965): 14.

3 Evelyn J.A. Evans, "Library Services in Ghana," in *Library Work in Africa*, ed. Wallenius, 17.

4 E.M. Broome, "Books for the People," 65-66.

5 Broome, "Books for the People," 69.

6 Broome, "Books for the People," 70.

The promise of the 1950s and 1960s has not been fulfilled in much of Africa. Proclaiming that they were saving their people from mismanagement and corruption, soldiers overthrew elected governments. The saviors proved most adept at holding onto power and at filling their own pockets. A few of the political rulers of the 1960s hung on until death or the multiparty movements of the 1990s finally brought them down. Superpower rivalry between the U.S. and the U.S.S.R. did harm in the Horn of Africa and elsewhere. The white South African regime worked to destabilize neighboring states that had a socialist ideology or were sympathetic to black majority rule at home. War and drought took their toll. Prices for African commodities continued to be set outside the continent. The World Bank and the International Monetary Fund achieved superpower influence. Literacy rates fell from 60 percent in 1980 to 52 percent in 1990.[7] Towards the end of the colonial era Kenneth Kaunda (later long-term president of Zambia) had recollected how, as a child in the 1920s, he had only been able to attend school, because a neighbor lent his mother the two shillings and six pence for the fees: "For so small a thing in those days could a child for ever forfeit the privilege of his life's education."[8] In the 1980s school fees were reintroduced in some of the countries that had abolished them earlier.

As times grew harder, the morale of public service staff in certain parts of Africa deteriorated. Even in better days those with an entrepreneurial spirit might try to supplement their salaries by renting out property, running a taxi service, or raising chickens to sell. Now a primary teacher might wait weeks or months for his overdue salary. As for public service library staff, they have no way of earning more than their salaries, with the exception of those few who use their say in the award of contracts to extract kickbacks or to sell donated books. A library that has not been able to pay for books and journals from other African countries or from overseas for more than a decade is not likely to provide a stimulating environment in which to work. Some libraries are now so poor in resources that they no longer buy even the local newspapers.

---

[7] UNESCO figures cited in Raseroka, "Changes in Public Libraries," 157.

[8] Extract from Kenneth David Kaunda, *Zambia Shall Be Free* (1962) in *Two Centuries of African English: A Survey of Non-Fictional English Prose by African Writers since 1769*, ed. Lalage Bown (London: Heinemann, 1973), 143.

War-torn Eritrea is an extreme example, but as many of the University of Asmara library staff as could manage to transferred to other units, where opportunities for training and promotion were better. The library became "a place for punishment or demotion" for those found guilty of misconduct elsewhere.[9]

The 1965 Scandinavian conference concluded that its deliberations had given rise to more questions than answers.[10] A similar conference today would have no difficulty in coming up with even more searching questions. It is coming up with answers that is the problem. Some issues, however, have remained in the forefront over the years, and a consideration of these, and of certain continuities from the colonial period to the present, will at least illuminate discussion.

What People Want to Read: News and Religious Material

Three categories stand out from all the rest: news, material containing a religious message or written from a religious point of view, and educational textbooks.

The little clusters of readers around roadside newspaper stands in the early morning are a daily reminder of people's interest in news. It was papers rather than books that attracted black South African readers in the nineteenth century, according to Mike Kantey.[11] Elspeth Huxley, whose fear of a "disaffected and irresponsible" press has already been mentioned, believed that each copy of an issue was read by as many as ten or twelve people.[12] The colonial authorities' nervousness about the power of the press has been exceeded by some of their successors. K.J. Mchombu and K. Miti maintain that African governments restrict access to information, because their actions are not always responsive or accountable to their people. They are insecure and they fear criticism. This negative

[9] Assefaw Abraha, "The Development of the University of Asmara Library," in *Survival Strategies in African University Libraries*, ed. Helga Atkinson Patrikios and Lisbeth A. Levey (Washington, D.C.: AAAS, 1994), 12.

[10] Gert Hornwall, "Concluding Remarks," in *Library Work in Africa*, ed. Wallenius, 72.

[11] Mike Kantey, "Publishing in South Africa," foreword to *Africa Bibliography 1986*, comp. Hector Blackhurst (Manchester: Manchester University Press, 1987), vii.

[12] Huxley, "Literature for Africans," pars. 20, 21.

attitude has various effects, one of which is the playing down of the information needs of the rural areas from which the government enlists local people for various schemes.[13]

Reservations about the content of newspapers rarely stops people from at least glancing through them, though a few will go to the extent of founding their own papers and newsletters to get a message across. Shiraz Durrani points out that in the 1930s the East African Trade Union Congress used cyclostyle machines to produce leaflets and handbills, which were distributed by bicycle. The *Mau Mau* continued such methods in the 1950s.[14] In the 1980s the organ of the guerrilla movement that was to overthrow the Milton Obote regime, the *Uganda Resistance News*, was also cyclostyled. According to its editor, publication depended on volunteers who sacrificed time, money, and sometimes their lives to ensure that it came out.[15] If people believe that certain news and beliefs are sufficiently important, they will endeavor to spread them, and an audience of listeners and readers will be found.

Christian missionaries taught East Africans to read "for the specific purpose of bringing them into a new relationship to a new knowledge—the knowledge of a religious faith," according to Charles Richards. Literacy was only a step in a process.[16] The first publication in many African languages was a section of the Bible. The publishing work of the CMS Bookshop, Nairobi, in the 1940s, has already been outlined. "Wisdom rather than knowledge, truth and not just facts," was given as the purpose of one Christian publishing house, Daystar, in the 1970s.[17] Modupe Oduyoye, its manager, said that the company had sold over 100,000 copies of *Friendship Between Boys and Girls* in

---

[13] Mchombu and Miti, "Formulation of National Information Policies," 167.

[14] Durrani, "Independence in Kenya," forthcoming.

[15] Cited in Shiraz Durrani, "The Mirage of Democracy in Kenya: People's Struggle for Information as an Aspect of the Struggle for Liberation" (paper presented at the "Emerging Democracies and Freedom of Information" conference of the International Group of the Library Association, Somerville College, Oxford, 2-4 September 1994).

[16] C.G. Richards, "Account of Problems in the Distribution of Literature for New Literates. Ref: Secretary of State's Savingram, Circular 321/57 of 14.3.57," PP.MS.12/59, Richards papers.

[17] Modupe Oduyoye, "The Role of Christian Publishing Houses in Africa Today," in *Publishing in Africa in the Seventies*, ed. Edwina Oluwasanmi, Eva McLean and Hans Zell (Ile-Ife: University of Ife Press, 1975), 224.

every English-speaking country in Africa. No teacher had ever recommended it, no classroom ever used it, but it was a success, he believed, because it met a need in the hearts of young people.[18] In K.J. Mchombu's recent study of two villages in Malawi, the Bible and hymn books turned out to form the most-read category of material. In one of the villages the Koran came next. The majority of the villagers were semiliterate, however, and over half of the respondents either read nothing or did not respond to the question.[19]

Religious publications are widely distributed, and a recent chairman of the Kenya Publishers Association, Henry Chakava, says that commercial publishers could learn from this success.[20] Financial help is sometimes received from churches overseas. Richards summed up the situation when he said that Christian publishers exist for what is in their books, not for what they can make out of them: "They feel that they have something to share."[21] Links between religion and politics are or have been close in some Islamic and Christian countries in Africa and elsewhere. Religious presses can come into conflict with the civil authorities, when their books, pamphlets, magazines, and newspapers—which may well provide more balanced coverage than government-controlled media—have political overtones. This makes people even more interested in reading them.

What People Want to Read: Educational Textbooks

The emphasis on education, on textbooks, and on the educational demands made on the public library is well documented. In the 1930s Foyles, the London bookshop, did a "very considerable cash trade" with West Africa, almost entirely in educational texts and theology (the "poorer type of private student" from the Gold Coast was the worst at

---

[18] Oduyoye, "Role of Christian Publishing Houses," 226.

[19] Kingo J. Mchombu, "Information Needs for Rural Development: The Case Study of Malawi," *African Journal of Library, Archives and Information Science* 2 (1992): 17-32.

[20] Henry Chakava, "Kenyan Publishing: Independence and Dependence," in *Publishing and Development in the Third World*, ed. Altbach , 130.

[21]Richards, "Interview,"164.

paying).[22] In 1941 all the teachers that Ethel Fegan met on the Gold Coast told her that a lending library would be "a great boon" to the country.[23] Visiting the Northern Rhodesia Copperbelt in 1943, Malcolm Guthrie found it not surprising that Africans regarded education as no more than "a means of monetary self-improvement;" why should they feel otherwise, when they saw that Europeans were there for their own financial benefit and using their knowledge for little more than that? "The value of any knowledge is estimated by the increase it brings in the size of one's pay envelope."[24] Fifty years later a librarian at the Copperbelt University, C.B.M. Lungu, described the reading habits of the public in developing societies such as Zambia as "so utilitarian that unless one has an academic undertaking one does not see the need to read anything at all."[25]

The Gold Coast had "vast numbers" of private students taking correspondence courses, Evans reported in 1956. They could not afford to buy all the books they needed. The Board found "great difficulty" in meeting the demand for textbooks but decided to provide a good supply of them in the reference libraries.[26] "Basic" books supplied to all branch libraries include the following out of the original list of well over a hundred titles: *Automobile Workshop Practice, Inorganic Chemistry, Modern Office Management, Economics for Students, The Social Framework, Teach Yourself Local Government,* and *A Gold Coast Geography.*[27] For the East African Literature Bureau lending textbooks was important, because "every assistance should be given to Africans to qualify," and again few could afford to buy.[28] In the early 1980s C.C. Aguolu described the

[22] Kaye Whiteman, ed., *West Africa over 75 Years: Selections from the Raw Material of History* (London: West Africa Publishing, [1993]), 44.

[23] "Carnegie Lending Library, Gold Coast: Miss Fegan's Report, March-June 1941," West Africa—Library Development 1936-1945 file, CCNY archives.

[24] Guthrie, "Report of an Investigation," 8.

[25] C.B.M. Lungu, "Review of Urban Public Library Educational Services (UPLES) in Kitwe, Zambia: A Survey," in *Proceedings of the Info Africa Nova Conference 1993,* vol. 1, ed. A.G. Coetzer (Pretoria: Info Africa Nova, 1993), 231.

[26] Evans, *Development of Public Library Services* , 20-22.

[27] Evans, *Tropical Library Service,* 166-70.

[28] "Outlines for Discussion Regarding the Development of the E.A. Literature Bureau Libraries Service—Kenya Section," no date [1953?], PP.MS.12/32e, Richards papers.

Borno State Library, Nigeria, as a reading room that served young adults from secondary schools and government workers preparing for examinations.[29] K.J. Mchombu says the differences between a public and a school library in Tanzania are so minor as to be almost nonexistent.[30] When Nelly Temu-Williams from Book Aid International visited the Dar es Salaam branch of the Tanzania Library Service in 1991, she found it packed with uniformed students: "One would have thought at first glance that this was a school library."[31]

The logical response to such demand is a textbook library. When the British Council moved into its premises in Harare in the early 1980s, it decided to use the basement to help meet the educational needs of ex-combatants: Zimbabweans whose formal education had been interrupted, when they took up arms against minority white Rhodesian rule. They needed to study in order to pass examinations, and the Council provided tables, chairs, and textbooks to read on the premises. John Salter, the Council's head of Library Services in Zimbabwe in the late 1980s and early 1990s, says that this was a case of the right facility in the wrong place: most users came from what are now called the high-density suburbs, the old African townships on the outskirts of the city. He encouraged municipal authorities to start other textbook collections, and the Council helped to stock them. One, with 150 seats, is open for ten hours a day, divided into five two-hour shifts. No seat is ever vacant.[32, 33]

The "book banks" set up by Makerere University in 1989 are lending rather than reference collections, and it is now the policy of the Uganda Ministry of Education and Sports to establish them in all tertiary institutions. Organized on a departmental basis by the university library, they contain

[29] C.C. Aguolu, "Libraries as Agents of Research and Scholarship, with Special Reference to Borno State," *Annals of Borno* 1 (1983), 22.

[30] K.J. Mchombu, "Alternatives to the National Library in Less Developed Countries," *Libri* 35 (1985), 230.

[31] Nelly Temu-Williams, "Report on a Visit to Tanzania, 11th-15th November 1991," BAI files.

[32] Telephone interview with John Salter, 11 October 1994.

[33] The Council later decided it needed its basement for other purposes, and the textbook collection is no longer there. The location of library collections brings to mind Kenya before independence, and the controversy as to whether they should be in the urban centers or the African locations. See Rosenberg, "The Colonial State," 141-42.

multiple copies of recommended texts. Students can borrow them for up to a year if they need to. The book banks contained around 114,000 volumes in 1993, according to Robert Davies, who says the authorities may see them as an alternative to libraries.[34]

Given the thirst for education, what part do school libraries play? A very limited one, because many amount to no more than shelves of dated and worn-out material, nominally supervised by a teacher who is too busy, too uninterested, or too ill-paid to pay much attention.[35] They are the poor of a library world that is not overabundant in riches. With such a large percentage of the population of Africa being made up of young people, this is little less than tragic. In his 1960 report Hockey summed up his visits to seventy-five mainly secondary level schools as "a most depressing experience." The book stock was inadequate and unsuitable, the accommodation poor. Not surprisingly the teachers were uninterested.[36] In their 1990 report on Zambia, Julie Carpenter and her colleagues summed up secondary school and teacher-training college libraries as "mainly responsive, passive elements" within their institutions. The buildings were run down, the furniture dilapidated, the books outdated and showing signs of "intensive and prolonged use." In addition there was "a high proportion of largely irrelevant donated books taking up shelf space which would otherwise be empty."[37] According to the Zambian librarian cited earlier, "Effectively there are no libraries in government schools in Kitwe." This is the country's second largest city, with a population estimated at over half a million people. Mismanagement, vandalism, and the fact that the collections are entirely dependent on book donations are among the problems.[38]

---

[34] Robert Davies, "Uganda," [Final report of the country focus group in the study conducted under the auspices of the International Library and Information Action for Development—Higher Education Information Development Research project], 1993, 18-20.

[35] However, a number of participants in the Black South African Teacher-Librarian course, held at Thames Valley University each Spring from 1988 to 1991, maintained that their schools had very good libraries, and they produced photographs to prove it.

[36] Hockey, "Development of Library Services in East Africa," appendix.

[37] Carpenter and others, "Book Sector in Zambian Education," 14.

[38] Lungu, "Review of Urban Public Library Educational Services," 234.

Paul Sturges and Richard Neill point out another hurdle. They maintain that African librarians themselves are less than fully convinced of the importance of librarianship for young people and do not in general place a high value on school libraries. Many African teachers are content to persist with the "rigid and sterile" teaching methods that they themselves experienced as children.[39] Many others, however, are more than anxious for books. One Zimbabwean headmaster wrote to Book Aid International about the "many untold problems" that his primary school was experiencing in trying to provide each child with a book to read. This school was situated in a large-scale farming area, and the pupils were the children of farm workers, many of whom were migrants from neighboring countries. Adult illiteracy was over 75 percent. The school, started by the farm owner in 1974, served as little more than a place in which to while away time up until 1990, when it was registered with the Ministry of Education and Culture. Then, when qualified teachers arrived, "they were met by large numbers of children hungry for education." One book had to be shared between twelve pupils. The parents tried their best, but with the 1992 drought they were "struggling to find the next meal for the same children." The farm owner tried, but his income went down when tobacco prices fell in 1993. The per capita grant from the government was insufficient for both exercise books and reading material. The headmaster wrote for help, his wish being "to see illiteracy . . . eradicated from these people."[40]

British teachers working in Africa under the auspices of Voluntary Service Overseas are often interested in establishing a school library, or in acquiring new material for one that already exists, and many call upon Book Aid International for help. Doris Lessing looked at one small library set up by a volunteer teacher in a rural part of Zimbabwe and noted that the books could not be taken home. There would be little point in doing so, she added, when the village would have no electricity, the walk to it would be long, and the children—the girls especially—would be expected to cut wood, fetch water,

[39] Sturges and Neill, *The Quiet Struggle*, 142.

[40] . . . to Book Aid International, 29 April 1994, Thank You Letters, Requests, Proposals N-Z 1994 file, BAI.

and cook. Homework had to be done at the school by the children before they left.[41] In addition to the need for books there is the need for a quiet, well-lit place in which to read them.

Some people also want to read recreational material. The African Writers series started by Heinemann in the 1960s became internationally famous. A lighter note was introduced, when Henry Chakava of Heinemann East Africa (later East African Educational Publishers) thought up Spear Books in the 1970s. Macmillan has had much success with Pacesetters, and Heinemann has recently launched African Heartbeats.[42] But news, religious material, and educational textbooks remain the basics, and all three would continue to be published, distributed, bought, and read in Africa if libraries were no more.

The Librarian as Obstacle

Observing the situation in Ghana in the early 1960s, Ronald Benge said that no one would dispute that textbooks and manuals were the essential reading matter.[43] In fact, numerous librarians molded in the Anglo-American tradition have spurned or played down textbook provision. Others have avoided having anything to do with the reading needs of new literates. A few, such as Kate Ferguson, have waged military-style campaigns to keep people out of their libraries—to keep the "wrong sort" of people out at any rate.

Joan Parkes (later Joan Allen), Northern Nigeria's first regional librarian, said she would not buy textbooks for her service. However, she was prepared to order personal copies for readers who would pay for them.[44] S.H. Horrocks, UNESCO consultant to the Eastern Nigeria regional library in the late 1950s, was pleased that no special attention was paid to providing textbooks. He felt that educated Nigerians should be reading imaginative literature, and that *Alice in Wonderland*

[41] Doris Lessing, *African Laughter: Four Visits to Zimbabwe* (London: Harper Collins, 1992), 204.

[42] Henry Chakava, "Private Enterprise Publishing in Kenya: A Long Struggle for Emancipation," *Logos* 4 (1993): 134.

[43] R.C. Benge, "Some Notes on Reading in Ghana," *Library World* 64 (1963), 210.

[44] "Libraries and the West African Community: A Talk Given . . . [by K. Middlemast] . . . with Notes on the Discussion," *WALA News* 2 (1955): 30.

or Jane Austen were more important than Simon's *Local Government*.[45] Irving Lieberman, who carried out the survey of the Lagos public library in 1963/64, recommended that the stock of readers or primers should not be replaced, when they wore out. They were basically school texts and public libraries do not provide school texts.[46]

Philip Rappaport, the Ford adviser who ran the National Library of Nigeria, insisted that only material from the library's own collections, or acquired on loan from another library, could be used in its reading rooms. Otherwise the library would become "yet another reading room filled with students preparing for examinations." This was not what a national library was supposed to be.[47] At the Queen Victoria Memorial Library, Salisbury, Rhodesia, in 1978 the reference librarian spent much of her time handing out textbooks and answering simple questions, which was "not really the work of a Reference Librarian." What made the situation worse was that the library had accumulated "an excellent collection of books which would enable us to assist anyone carrying out serious research."[48] Benge summed up such situations as follows: "Clearly the readers are expected to exist for the sake of the library instead of the other way round."[49]

Dawn E. Evenden, who has been on the staff of the Johannesburg Public Library for more than forty years, says that it has never been library policy to purchase textbooks, although supplementary material is acquired to help students. In the 1990s, however, more and more of those who use the Young Adults' Reference Library are studying by correspondence and regard the library as their school. The correspondence colleges do little more than provide duplicated sets of notes, yet they, not the libraries, have the staff who are trained to teach. A time came, when it seemed that students might completely take over the adult Reference Library itself. The library's solution to

[45] S.H. Horrocks, "Eastern Region and UNESCO Public Library Pilot Project," *WALA News* 3 (1958): 14.

[46] Lieberman, *Survey of the Lagos City Library*, 55-56.

[47] Rappaport, *Libraries and Library Development in Nigeria*, 40.

[48] Queen Victoria Memorial Library Salisbury, Rhodesia, "Report for the Year Ended 31st December 1978," 4.

[49] Ronald Charles Benge, *Cultural Crisis and Libraries in the Third World* (London: Clive Bingley, 1979), 203.

this was to set aside some space for "the general public," with the rest for students, who might not use the other seats. Student seats are numbered, and students receive a token with their seat number from the staff member who sits at the entrance. But there is a permanent queue to get in. This misleads members of the public who see the queue and think there are no seats. It frustrates the lined-up students who see empty seats but are not permitted to sit on them. The library has made other efforts, however. It turned a meeting room into an unsupervised study area (also always crowded) and provided extra reading space for students in the new Eldorado Park branch library. Evenden says that there is no money to alter the main library in such a way as to provide more space, and that, given the increasing number of students, it is debatable whether there would ever be enough space anyway. She says the educational authorities should pay attention to the problem.[50]

To suggest that librarians were conscious of being obstacles in the paths of nonliterates and new literates would be to exaggerate, but it is fair to say that not many have gone out of their way to help. At the 1953 Ibadan UNESCO seminar a young Nigerian librarian, Gbole N. Nwikina, supplied one of the best reasons that can be put forward for wanting to learn to read and write: to avoid being cheated by one's literate brother and by the community.[51] The seminar participants who were really enthusiastic about the link between libraries and literacy programs were those such as Charles Richards, a committed Christian who considered banishing illiteracy to be part of the duty of the Church.[52] The enthusiasm for the role libraries might play petered out over the years in much of Africa. Dennis Gunton, Allen's successor as regional librarian of Northern Nigeria, believes that this was not deliberate. Rather, the enormity of the task was intuitively recognized and left to university primary education to tackle. He points out

---

[50] Dawn E. Evenden, "The Johannesburg Public Library: A Personal View of Some of the Events of the Last Fifteen Years," in *A World Too Wide: Essays on Libraries and Other Themes in Honour of Reuben Musiker,* ed. Joseph Sherman (Johannesburg: University of the Witwatersrand Library, 1993), 115-16.

[51] Gbole N. Nwikina, "Reading Habits of Nigerians," in *Development of Public Libraries in Africa: The UNESCO Seminar* (Paris: UNESCO, 1954), 71.

[52] C.G. Richards, "Literature in the Life and Work of the Church: A Paper for the First Provincial Synod, August 1960," PP.MS.12/58, Richards papers.

that the background and qualifications of the small band of librarians did not equip them for the work.[53]   In his recommendations for Northern Nigeria in 1963, F.A. Sharr said public libraries were not suitable agencies for meeting the needs of new literates, although it would be appropriate for them to answer specific questions or provide simple information verbally.[54] "Shoot them" was one Nigerian librarian's jocular response to a conference question about what should be done for the illiterate.[55] Charles Richards, reflecting back in 1975 on forty years association with adult literacy, described it as "the Cinderella among the social services . . . a despised and neglected sister."[56]

Distribution

When there is not a great deal to spread around, it is harder to work out how best to distribute it. "In tatters and hopelessly over-extended anyway," was a Zimbabwean's 1992 description of his country's library service, "which frankly doesn't exist outside urban centres."[57] In the 1950s the East African Literature Bureau had wanted its new postal service to reach out to people in isolated areas. After several years lack of government support forced it to increase charges and close its membership register. According to S.K. Ng'ang'a, the postal service of one of its successors, the Kenya National Library Service, was down to seven members in 1990.[58] The Gold Coast Library Board used to do better. "Books to the People" was its motto, and it started a postal service for teachers. It provided a mobile service and branch libraries in temporary premises before putting up "prestige buildings."[59] The Tanzania Library Service thought it essential to have buildings in place before mobiles could be put into operation. In the 1970s the National

[53] Dennis Gunton to author, 16 November 1984.

[54] *Library Needs of Northern Nigeria,* 111.

[55] Cited in Ronald Benge, "Return to West Africa: Some Notes on Library Education in Africa," *Nigerian Libraries* 9 (1973): 98.

[56] "Report of Visit to ALOR (Adult Literacy Organisation of Rhodesia) March to July 1975," 7, PP.MS.12/108a, Richards papers.

[57] . . . to Book Aid International, 4 March 1992, Zimbabwe General 1993 file, BAI.

[58] Cited in Rosenberg, "Imposing Libraries," 36.

[59] Evans, "Library Services in Ghana," 7-8.

Library of Nigeria took the novel step of opening branches in some state capitals.

In a criticism of what he called the Taj Mahal complex in 1984, K.J. Mchombu pointed out that for every library built to Anglo-American standards one could build twenty cheaper ones using mud bricks. The walls could be plastered and whitewashed and inexpensive furniture provided. In this way twenty times as many people could be reached.[60] The problem, however, is that many of those reached would be likely to fall away again, unless a certain basic level (which includes keeping the library open during the hours it is supposed to be open) is maintained. Past experience is not encouraging. Despairing of improving the standard of the reading rooms throughout Northern Nigeria, the regional library service drew back and concentrated on the capital, Kaduna. The East African Literature Bureau gave up on book boxes, switching its efforts to static collections instead: "Only larger well-organised libraries are worth the time and labour."[61] In 1960 S.W. Hockey concluded that there was a level below which it was better not to attempt to provide a service at all.[62] The Bureau was disappointed with the local supervisors of its book box collections.

The Ghana Library Board had a similar experience with the honorary librarians of its rural library centers. According to D.E.M. Oddoye these were mainly teachers "whose main interest had been to seize the opportunity to obtain textbooks for self-improvement." The centers were often closed, when they should have been open. In 1974 the Board decided to upgrade all of them to full-time branches run by its own staff.[63] More recently, writing about individual rural libraries set up as a result of local initiative or foreign aid, Diana Rosenberg points out that only a stable and continuing administrative structure can provide them with long-term sustenance. She believes that history and financial problems prevent the public

---

[60] K.J. Mchombu, "Development of Library and Documentation Services in Tanzania: Problems of Strategy and Tactics," *Information Processing and Management* 20 (1984): 564.

[61] EALB, *Annual Report 1960-61*, 4.

[62] Hockey, "Development of Library Services in East Africa," par. 1(1).

[63] D.E.M. Oddoye, "Ghana Library Board," in *Aspects of African Librarianship*, ed. Michael Wise (London and New York: Mansell, 1985), 81.

library service from providing this, but that local nongovernmental organizations (NGOs) such as churches offer possibilities.[64]

Mobile services tend not to last. There will be no fuel or no money for fuel. The vehicle will break down, and there will be no spare parts. Other government vehicles will break down, and the library one will either be commandeered or cannibalized. The library driver will be requisitioned for work rated more important than delivering books, or he will be transferred and find himself driving a high-ranking official.

The Bureau had a vehicle that was a combined bookshop and library. It delivered books to the library centers and permitted members of the postal library service to borrow books from its shelves. The Bureau concluded that "if only it were possible to take the library books around the country, the use made of the library services would be tremendous."[65] Yet, a few years later the vehicle was immobilized, because the money allocated for travel had been reduced. By 1976 three of the Tanzania Library Service's rural mobile libraries had broken down completely, leaving only two on the road.[66] The Sierra Leone Library Board received two Landrover-type mobile libraries from the British Council in 1980. Fuel costs and bad roads took their toll, and the mobile service to primary schools had to be suspended in 1983/84.[67] By 1987 the Ghana Library Board's mobile library service had ceased.[68] James M. Ng'ang'a told a seminar in Nairobi in 1993 that the Kenya National Library Service "also [had] a number of mobile libraries which, however, have not moved for the last year or two."[69]

[64]Diana Rosenberg, "Rural Community Resource Centres: A Sustainable Option for Africa?" *Information Development* 9 (1993): 34.

[65] EALB, *Annual Report 1957-58*, 4.

[66] C.S. Ilomo, "The History and Work of Tanzania Library Service 1963-80," in *Aspects of African Librarianship*, ed. Wise , 132.

[67] Gloria E. Dillsworth, "The Sierra Leone National Public Library Service," in *Information and Libraries in the Developing World*, vol. 1, *Sub-Saharan Africa*, ed. Michael Wise and Anthony Olden (London: Library Association, 1990), 115.

[68] *Ghana: Libraries and Information Profile 1987* (London: British Council, 1987), 2.

[69] James M. Ng'ang'a, "Reading at Home and How to Develop Home Libraries," in *Children's Reading Needs: The Challenges of the Next Century to Parents, Educators, Publishers and Librarians in Africa*, ed. Serah W. Mwanycky (Nairobi: CHISCI Press, 1993), 25.

Technology

The impact that new technology is having in some African academic and research libraries is documented in the proceedings of a workshop that took place at the University of Zimbabwe in August 1993. The event was organized by the university and the American Association for the Advancement of Science and paid for by the Ford Foundation. The two CD-ROM workstations, laser jet printer, and the initial subscriptions to two CD-ROM databases that Carnegie Corporation of New York money had brought to the University of Dar es Salaam were discussed by John M. Newa. Was there sufficient expertise in Tanzania to maintain the technology, he asked? And how could the library ensure that the service would continue after overseas support would end? It had, in fact, made a start on this by requiring users to pay for printouts and document delivery, and by including hardware, software, database subscriptions, and document delivery expenses in its computer and journal budgets. Newa said that the content of some databases was not especially relevant to Tanzania, that lack of heavy-duty photocopy machines caused problems, and that students and lecturers had shown less interest than anticipated, so that additional marketing and promotion were required.[70] Margaret Ngwira (Bunda College of Agriculture, Malawi) asked whether a good computer information system should be ranked a success or a failure, when it was paid for entirely from outside the country.[71] Helga Atkinson Patrikios said that microcomputer and CD-ROM technology were well-established at the University of Zimbabwe Medical Library.[72]

Electronic mail is now a possibility at some universities, but computer conferencing has yet to arrive. A computer conference on measuring the impact of information on development was organized by the International Development Research Centre

---

[70] John M. Newa, "The Sustainability of Information Technology Innovations: CD-ROM at the University of Dar es Salaam," in *Survival Strategies,* ed. Patrikios and Levey, 77-83.

[71] Margaret Ngwira, "Information Delivery in Malawi with Special Emphasis on the Bunda College of Agriculture Library," in *Survival Strategies,* ed. Patrikios and Levey, 88.

[72] Helga Atkinson Patrikios, "A Minimal Acquisitions Policy for Journals at the University of Zimbabwe Medical Library," in *Survival Strategies,* ed. Patrikios and Levey, 95.

(IDRC), Ottawa, in 1992. No member of the core group of sixteen specialists selected to participate by IDRC was based in Africa, an odd omission given how central the continent is to the development debate. This appears to have been due to "lack of adequate telecommunication facilities."[73] Was this a situation in which the content of the message mattered less than did access to the technology chosen for communication? Later on, however, the IDRC did select a group of thirteen specialists to form a consultative panel, and two of the thirteen were Africans. A third African participated in the post-conference workshop. This was Betty Bigombe, a Ugandan government minister, who spoke on "the role, value, and limitations of information for those at the highest levels of policy- and decision-making."[74]

   "If there is a single weapon that will help in the struggle to keep information alive and well in Africa, it is certainly the PC," stated F.W.G. Hill, pro-vice-chancellor of the University of Zimbabwe, at the opening of the 1993 workshop.[75] Technology is indeed having an impact, but it does need to be paid for, just as books, journals, and newspapers do. It also requires technical expertise to keep it functioning. Sadly, it is hardly likely that public and school libraries in most of Africa are likely to have much access to it, given the level of support they receive. And it will be some years yet before villagers in the bush communicate via the Internet.

Local Publishing

Russell Bowden believes that Book Aid International's work can only be "a stop-gap" for the problems of library development in Africa: "In the end the solution has got to lie in indigenous publishing."[76]

---

73 Michel J. Menou, ed., *Measuring the Impact of Information on Development* (Ottawa: International Development Research Centre, 1993), 5. The membership information is taken from the list of names amongst the appendices.

74 Menou, *Measuring the Impact*, 84.

75 F.W.G. Hill, "Strategic Planning for University Libraries: Welcome to Workshop Participants," in *Survival Strategies*, ed. Patrikios and Levey, 9.

76 "Enhanced Credibility" [Interview with Russell Bowden], *Library Association Record* 96 (1994): 212. Bowden, former deputy chief executive of the British Library Association, served on the Council of Book Aid for a number of years. His ties with Africa include a number of years on the staff of the British Council, Nigeria, in the early 1970s.

The development of local publishing is indeed important,[77] but it will not benefit libraries, if they are without the money with which to buy its products. Local publications and those from other African countries ought to provide the bulk of library stock, but total self-sufficiency is never likely to be possible. The United Kingdom imports books, despite publishing 78,835 titles (including reprints and new editions) in 1992.[78] The African Publishers Network (APNET) points out that, if Kenya and Zimbabwe, two model publishing countries in the African context, are taken together, their book market size, expressed in monetary terms, is less than one-twentieth of a European country with a smaller population such as Norway, Denmark, or the Netherlands.[79] School textbooks are where the money is: children, parents, and teachers are well aware of their importance and willing to make sacrifices to obtain them. Some commercial publishers have had their share of this market reduced or eliminated. This was brought about first through government and then through World Bank involvement in book provision.

At the Commonwealth Conference in London in 1963 Kwame Nkrumah told British publisher Harold Macmillan (who had recently stepped down as prime minister) that he wanted Ghanaian schoolbooks for his country but lacked the expertise to produce them. Macmillan said that his company would assist, and the outcome was the Ghana Publishing Corporation, a joint venture between that company and the Nkrumah government. Macmillan also entered into agreements with Tanzania, Uganda, and Zambia. The new parastatal organizations had the monopoly on publishing primary schoolbooks. There was little local publishing in these ex-colonies at the time, and British firms historically had a monopoly on the supply of English-language material. The other British publishers that used to supply the market up to then were angry at being out-maneuvred. In most instances,

---

[77] And, as has been mentioned in Chapter 2, Book Aid and the African Books Collective are involved with it through the Intra African Book Support Scheme.

[78] *Euromonitor Book Report 1993* (London: Euromonitor, 1993), 6.

[79] [African Publishers Network], "Approaches to Book Provision in Africa: The APNET Perspective. A Synthesis of Major Issues with Recommendations . . . for Submission to the World Bank in Support of the APNET Visit . . . 8th to 10th December 1993," 7.

however, although the parastatals continued to operate, their
connection with Macmillan did not last very long. Alan Hill of
Heinemann Educational Books believes that this was not
because of inadequacies in the plan, but because local conditions
did not enable Macmillan to do the job properly, with the result
that "the children didn't get the right books at the right price
at the right time."[80]

The idea of one national organization producing and
supplying all the schoolbooks a country needed had its
attractions. It was to reduce and then eliminate foreign
involvement, with its overtones of cultural dependency and its
concern that profits be repatriated. It was to provide children
with texts written by their own people; who could interpret
their countries and their continent better? It was to put an end to
wasteful duplication and competition. In practice, however,
things did not always work out quite so well. There was no
profit incentive. Large numbers of people were employed by the
parastatals, but not all were productively employed.
Bureaucratic procedures slowed things down. Writing, editing,
design, and production took longer than should have been the
case. Sometimes the product was poor. Usually the distribution
was unsatisfactory.

The World Bank's involvement with education and the
supply of textbooks has lured back to Africa the British firms
that stayed out of the way, when the foreign exchange dried
up. As Charles McGregor points out, these multinationals are in
a stronger position to tender for World Bank contracts, because
they have associate or subsidiary companies locally. They may
attract better staff with more attractive conditions of service.
They may be able to secure better terms for paper and print,
because they buy in such bulk. They are in a position to call on
associates in other countries for titles that are capable of
adaptation for a new local curriculum.[81] Julie Carpenter and
her colleagues have pointed out the difference between getting
books into schools and developing the local printing industry. If
the former is the priority, then the printing should be done
"anywhere in the world where price, quality, reliability and

---

[80] Alan Hill, *In Pursuit of Publishing* (London: John Murray, 1988), 237.

[81] Charles McGregor, "Raiding the World Bank," *Bookseller*, 15 July 1994, 32-33.

delivery dates are as required."[82] In the same way the return of the multinationals gets books to schoolchildren but does little for local publishing. APNET has told the World Bank that African publishers are a "largely untapped and growing resource . . . . They have survived exasperating conditions and are operating nowhere near their potential."[83]

School textbooks are the lucrative market. At the other extreme are academic and professional journals, which have little chance of being published at a profit in Africa. Professional associations were established in the 1950s, often on a regional basis. These later split into associations organized nationally. The Ghana and the Nigerian Library Associations developed out of the West African Library Association. The *Ghana Library Journal* and *Nigerian Libraries* took over from *WALA News*. At first all went well, but then difficulties began to arise. In some instances these turned into insurmountable obstacles. No issue of the *Ghana Library Journal* appeared between 1973 and 1988, when it was resurrected.[84] *Maktaba,* the journal of the Kenya Library Association, and *Nigerian Libraries* have also had their problems, though less severe. Regular appearance becomes well-nigh impossible when the number of paid-up members is limited (even in a country as large as Nigeria). Telephone and mail communications are poor, which means that the taking over of responsibility, files and bank account by a new editor poses practical difficulties, when his predecessor is based seven or eight hundred miles away. Numerous other demands on the time of an editor impinge on work that is being done on a part-time basis anyway.[85] Academic journals may fare little better. The December 1979 issue of *Savanna: A Journal of the Environmental and Social Sciences* appeared in 1987. The publishers, Ahmadu Bello University Press (Nigeria) Ltd., regretted the inconvenience (the company had been closed down for reorganization) and expressed their appreciation for "the understanding and

---

82 Carpenter and others, "The Books Sector in Zambian Education," 37.

83 [APNET], "Approaches to Book Provision in Africa," 3.

84 "Editorial," *Ghana Library Journal* 6 (1988): vii.

85 A good treatment of the situation will be found in *Survival Under Adverse Conditions: Proceedings of the African Library Science Journals Workshop,* ed. Michael Wise (The Hague: International Federation of Library Associations and Institutions, 1994).

continued cooperation of subscribers."[86]   Another example from Nigeria is *Kano Studies: A Bayero University Journal of Savanna and Sudanic Research.* Volume 2 number 3 of the new series is dated 1982/85. Academic and professional journals, like libraries, are not fundamental to education in Africa in the way that textbooks are. When times are hard they wither.

---

[86] "Publisher's Note to Subscribers," *Savanna: A Journal of the Environmental and Social Sciences* 8 (1979): ii. The author compiled the "Current Bibliography for the Savanna States on Nigeria" for the twice-yearly *Savanna* from 1977 to 1980, when it was obvious that the journal was in difficulties. When the December 1979 issue finally appeared nine years had elapsed since its "Current Bibliography" had been compiled.

Conclusion

At the opening of the Accra Central Library in 1956, Kwame Nkrumah, then Gold Coast prime minister, was in reflective mood. He recalled that it had not been common to attend school in rural villages such as the one in which he spent his childhood. But his parents forced him to, until one day he discovered that he rather enjoyed it. When he progressed on to Achimota College, he took with him his little library of three books: the Bible, Shakespeare's *Works*, and Alcock's *Grammar*. Later, in his "struggling days" in London, he could say without doubt that his "happiest hours were spent browsing among the books in the British Museum." When the Library Board approached him for money, he saw to it that it was made available, "and nobody who is here today can deny that that money was put to good use."[1] In 1964, in her *Tropical Library Service*, Evelyn Evans said that without the support of Nkrumah and his government, little could have been accomplished.[2] In his introduction Edward Sydney, the British public librarian who had led the UNESCO seminar at Ibadan in 1953, said that the book read like "a fairy story of dreams come true."[3]

In 1979 the president of Tanzania, Julius Nyerere, wrote that to develop an educational system and then say that one could not afford a national library service was not very sensible: "For poor nations a library service is vital."[4] Tanzania had been the East African country to make most progress with public library

[1] Nkrumah's speech is reproduced in Evans, *Tropical Library Service*, 48-50.

[2] Evans, *Tropical Library Service*, acknowledgements

[3] Edward Sydney in Evans, *Tropical Library Service*, xvii.

[4] Julius K. Nyerere, foreword to E.E. Kaungamno and C.S. Ilomo, *Books Build Nations*, vol. 1, *Library Services in East and West Africa* (London and Dar es Salaam: Transafrica Book Distributors and Tanzania Library Service, 1979).

development in the 1960s. Charles Richards says that Nyerere had always taken an interest in the work of the East African Literature Bureau, and that through his influence money was made available for libraries.[5]

In matters like these Nkrumah and Nyerere were far from typical of politicians or civil servants. The Kenya director of education was summed up by Malcolm Guthrie in 1943 as a time-server who was not really interested in education at all, but only in his own reputation.[6] The director of the Literature Bureau received the following message from a senior government officer: "Tell Charles Richards I have no money for books, I have to provide for training and equipping an army."[7] After independence Tom Mboya, a prominent Kenyan politician, said that "scholarships for librarians, when engineers are needed, are a waste of time."[8] Some politicians are quick to order books (particularly textbooks for schools) but slow to pay for them. In a 1991 paper Victor U. Nwankwo pointed out that Nigerian publishers were still owed debts of 42.3 million naira for books ordered by state governments during the 1979 to 1983 period of civilian rule. Needless to say, no interest was being paid on the debts.[9] In the early 1970s the Idi Amin regime in Uganda claimed no responsibility for paying for books supplied to the government of Milton Obote, which it had overthrown.[10]

According to David Clow, extracting money from those who control the purse strings is akin to getting blood out of a stone. One must learn to speak their language, which is "conservative, self-interested, finance-based, highly politics-conscious, minimum-

---

[5] Richards, *No Carpet*.

[6] Guthrie, "Report of an Investigation," 57. Sir Angus Gillan instructed that this part of the report was not to leave the office without his express approval. Gillan to Ward Price, 15 June 1944, BW7/1, PRO.

[7] Richards, *No Carpet*.

[8] Cited in Rosenberg, *The Colonial State*, 175.

[9] Victor U. Nwankwo, "Publishing in Nigeria Today," in *Publishing and Development in the Third World*, ed. Altbach, 160.

[10] Richards, "Tour Report, 6 June [1973]," PP.MS.12/98, Richards papers. As director of the Christian Literature Fund and of its successor, the Agency for Christian Literature Development, Richards kept a record of his travels. He continued to take an interest in book supply in East Africa, and was told about the payment problem by the Nairobi-based representative of a U.K. publisher.

risk, minimum-effort, maximum-gain, [and] protocol-ridden."[11] The language is the same in both developing and developed worlds, as is the fact that libraries are marginal, "a pleasant modest luxury on the fringes of serious activity."[12] This is an exaggeration for those parts of the world where libraries—or at any rate certain types of libraries—are strongly entrenched: the West, the former Communist world, and a number of developing countries such as China. But Clow's point is a valuable antidote to the grandiose assertions of some librarians. So is Kingo Mchombu's criticism of the profession for confusing a policy for libraries, archives, and documentation centers with a national information policy.[13] Similarly, Diana Rosenberg has pointed out that libraries alone do not satisfy information needs.[14] Douglas Waples, a professor at the University of Chicago's Graduate Library School in the 1930s, described them as "simply one instrumentality in the communication process."[15]

What libraries are good at is supporting education and research. Some governments in Africa are leaving this support, or as much of it as possible, to the mercy of foreigners. The contrast with China is striking. Up until 1992, when it joined the Berne Convention and the Universal Copyright Convention, China was busily translating foreign books without the permission or even the knowledge of their authors. Foreign serials such as *Biological Abstracts* would be reproduced in the hundreds or thousands and distributed to libraries without their publishers' permission. Software copying was widespread. Such practices drew the wrath of foreign publishers and authors and of foreign governments (the United States in particular), and threats of trade sanctions prodded China into signing the international

---

[11] David Clow, "Blood from Stones: A Polemic on the Funding of Library Services in Third World Countries," in *Nothing to Read? The Crisis of Document Provision in the Third World*, ed. D.J. Membrey (Edgbaston [Birmingham]: International and Comparative Librarianship Group of the Library Association, 1990), 105-6.

[12] Clow, "Blood from Stones," 98.

[13] Kingo Mchombu, "Which Way African Librarianship?" *IFLA Journal* 17 (1991): 35.

[14] Rosenberg, *The Colonial State*, 140.

[15] Cited in Blaise Cronin, Review of John V. Richardson, Jr., *The Gospel of Scholarship* (1992), *International Journal of Information and Library Research* 5 (1993): 62.

copyright agreements.[16] But such activities, unconventional though they were, did at least indicate China's belief that certain information was worth having, and the country made great strides in science and technology. By contrast, and "when measured in world terms," as Mchombu and Miti put it, "Africa's lack of scientific and technological development is frightening."[17] Writing about scientific and technical information in Ghana, A.A. Alemna says that the greatest obstacle to its use is the fact that decision makers and top government officials do not recognize its value.[18]

Money from outside of Africa helped to set up the McMillan Library in Nairobi, the Lagos Library, the East African Literature Bureau, and the National Library of Nigeria. The Northern Nigeria Regional Library, the Tanzania Library Service, and the Kenya National Library Service all received help with buildings, books, or staff training from Britain, Denmark, or other countries. Yet, the old donors are still donating, however their aims, projects, and techniques may have modified over the years. The Carnegie Corporation of New York and the Ford Foundation now back the efforts of the American Association for the Advancement of Science Project for African Research Libraries, which aims to improve access to scientific and technical information for African researchers. For the Carnegie Corporation this is another stage in its on-off involvement with library development in Africa since the 1920s. For the Ford Foundation the connection is more recent, dating from the heady days of independence. Book Aid's International Campus Book Link program may be new and very professional, but Ranfurly's philanthropic work goes back to the 1950s. Acknowledging its gifts in 1962-63, the East African Literature Bureau said that, although they alleviated to a slight extent

---

16 *Biological Abstracts* was one of the reproduced serials noticed by the author in a scientific library in a provincial capital in 1991. For more information on China and copyright see David Wei Ze, "China about to Join Copyright Conventions, but Writers Remain 'Vendors of Words'," *Logos* 3 (1992): 81-85; and Charles Oppenheim, "China's Intellectual Property Rights and Scientific and Technical Information Services," *Aslib Proceedings* 45 (1993): 261-66.

17 Mchombu and Miti, "Formulation of National Information Policies," 163.

18 A.A. Alemna, "Scientific and Technical Information in Ghana," *Information Development* 8 (1992): 219.

the book hunger of the young people of the area, they could not take the place of an organized public library service, which must be built into any program of educational and community development.[19] Some questions need to be asked. For how long more is outside aid going to be necessary or indeed appropriate? And, if the information—or part of it—that is supplied is felt to be of value, when are the holders of the purse strings in the recipient countries going to assume responsibility for paying for it—or part of it—themselves?

The role of American private philanthropic organizations in extending the influence of the West has already been mentioned. Aid from governments and government cultural and information-type organizations may focus more sharply on gaining or retaining influence or on sales potential. As Sidney Hockey remarked to a British Council colleague in 1968, British books were "one of our greatest assets in the ideological war."[20] As two British Council staff members put it in 1994, "The student studying the British textbook about widgets . . . later becomes the industrialist who buys British-made widgets."[21] Aid from Scandinavian countries is likely to be more neutral, a wish to assist people less fortunate by helping to provide things that Scandinavians themselves find of value at home: literacy, adult education, books, and libraries. Book Aid International is neutral, although for historic reasons it concentrates on the Commonwealth countries of Africa. However, Book Aid has contacts with the British Council and receives financial support from the Overseas Development Administration. A 1994 ODA review found its work to be "entirely consistent with the developmental and political objectives of HMG [Her Majesty's Government]."[22]

Aid professionals and consultants are often shrewd observers, well aware of what Carol Priestley (International African Institute/Swedish Agency for Research Cooperation with

---

[19] EALB, *Annual Report 1962-1963*, 1-2.

[20] Hockey to R.A. Flood, 26 August 1968, British Council file CL/GEN/265/14b, cited in Coombs, *Spreading the Word*, 176.

[21] Brigid O'Connor and Stephan Roman, "Building Bridges with Books: The British Council's Sixty-Year Record," *Logos* 5 (1994): 137.

[22] William Taylor, "A Review of ODA Support to the Ranfurly Library Service (Book Aid International)," 1994.

Developing Countries [SAREC]) calls the inherent dangers of what some donor organizations are doing. Material from "the North" may jeopardize the prospects of publishers in "the South," and donations may make librarians and researchers so dependent that they rely on foreign journals rather than attempt to produce their own.[23] One then has what Mchombu and Miti call consumption orientation, not the production orientation that is really needed.[24] Lisbeth A. Levey (AAAS) says the University of Ibadan Medical Library has drawn up a core list of 120 journals, but plans to subscribe to 400 when the World Bank loan to Nigerian universities comes into effect. She wonders not whether these 400 titles are important, but whether the university might not be better off maintaining a smaller core collection over a longer period of time.[25]

Sara Harrity (Book Aid International) wrote to thank a Kenyan government minister for a gift and for making a special visit to Nairobi to see her when she was there. She went on to say that, while her organization was delighted to be working with the Kenya National Library Service and other institutions, "I very much hope that it will be possible for the Kenya government to increase its provision for the local purchase of books in order to help develop the excellent publishing industry that exists in Kenya, and at the same time provide Kenyan children and adults with books produced in their own country."[26] In their 1990 consultancy report on Zambia, Julie Carpenter and her colleagues concluded that donations had taken the pressure off central authorities and school principals to maintain some level of recurrent library funding.[27]

When the reduction in the financial support given to libraries by their own authorities is taken together with the extremely small percentage of the African population actually receiving service, the result is a big question mark over the future of these libraries. Michael Casey, in a paper on the electronic information

[23] Carol Priestley, *SAREC Library Support Programme. Evaluation and Review: Ethiopia, Mozambique and Tanzania* (Stockholm: SAREC, 1993), 71.

[24] Mchombu and Miti, "Formulation of National Information Policies," 146.

[25] Levey, *Profile of Research Libraries*, 19-20.

[26] Sara Harrity to . . . , 1 October 1991, Kenya—General file, BAI.

[27] Carpenter and others, "The Books Sector in Zambian Education," 28.

industry in Europe, defined real information needs as what people are prepared to pay for.[28] It is obvious that some countries are badly off financially, and that food, water, shelter, medical care, communications, transport, armaments for security, and other basics have to take precedence. But a certain level of information and education is necessary, if there is to be progress and development, and evidence of a willingness to pay or to continue to pay for the library as a part of this is limited. One 1994 request for assistance to Book Aid International came from the librarian of an institute of public administration in a capital city. The library was being used by magistrates, state auditors, police prosecutors, personnel workers, and other civil servants. "So these donations benefit the country a lot . . . . This type of help through donations is very important to a government institution such as ours because funding by government is usually very minimal."[29] Why is it so minimal, if the information in the library is of such benefit to the country?

If librarians have not been sufficiently persuasive in arguing the value of information and libraries, neither do government ministers, members of parliament, army officers, or civil servants appear to have become persuaded through their own use of libraries in the past. Many graduated from African universities fifteen, twenty, or thirty years ago, when these possessed good library collections. Some studied overseas at universities which have very good libraries indeed. Ronald Benge says that, "Like illiteracy, overpopulation, or epidemics, the absence of reliable information is symptom of underdevelopment," and that the end result is silence.[30] Some of the present leaders and administrators are colluding in a silence that they themselves did not experience while at school or university. They hinder the development of local publishing by not removing paper and printing equipment from the list of imports to be taxed. They allocate scarce foreign exchange for videocassette recorders and plastic wastepaper baskets (when local craftsmen make perfectly

---

[28] Michael Casey, "The Electronic Information Industry in Europe: An Analysis of Trends and Prospects in Less Developed Economies," *Journal of Librarianship and Information Science* 23 (1991): 27.

[29] The source of this application is not being disclosed to preserve confidentiality.

[30] Benge, *Cultural Crisis*, 201.

good baskets with local materials), but not for agricultural journals. The library service to the elite and the would-be elite during the colonial and post-colonial periods seems to have done little to make the recipients more supportive, after they themselves completed their formal studies and largely ceased to use the libraries. Referring to libraries and adult education, the African Publishers Network says, "It is clear that the political will to uplift these two areas and utilize them as tools of national development is largely absent."[31] Mchombu and Miti also point out that African governments see information as a source of power rather than as a tool for development.[32]

The educational role of the library in Africa is the one that all the evidence attests to. People want the textbooks that will help them pass their examinations; they want supplementary material that will help them improve their performance; and they want quiet, well-lit space in which they can study and read. Individuals, parents and communities will do their best to pay for this on a local level at least, because they believe it will bring them practical returns. Assistance and advice from outside the locality will be necessary, because selection will be required, and books in constant use will wear out rapidly and need to be replaced. Newspapers, magazines, books for young people, other local publications, and if possible, material from other African countries and material about Africa published outside the continent will add to the interest. Although both past and present caution against overoptimism, centering library development on education does seem certain to produce the most dependable results.

---

31 [APNET], "Approaches to Book Provision in Africa," 10.

32 Mchombu and Miti, "Formulation of National Information Policies," 142.

Sources and Bibliography

Interviews

Evelyn J.A. Evans (former director, Ghana Library Board), 20 April 1988 (and subsequent conversations)

David Membrey (deputy director, Book Aid International), 10 August 1993 (and other conversations)

Marydee Ojala (former assistant vice-president and manager, Information Services, Bank of America, San Francisco), 8 September 1993 (telephone)

C.G. Richards (former director, East African Literature Bureau), 24 April 1993

Mary Ross-Smith (chief librarian, Harare City Library), 16 September 1994

John Salter (former head of Library Services, British Council, Zimbabwe, and former regional librarian, British Council, Southern Africa), 11 October 1994 (telephone)

Archives and Records

Book Aid International, London
Archive; Thank You Letters, Requests, Proposals; and Visits files; and current files on Ghana, Kenya, Malawi, Nigeria, Sierra Leone, Tanzania, Uganda, Zambia, and Zimbabwe

British Council Records in the Public Record Office, London
BW2/93 British Cultural Propaganda in West Africa (1941)
BW7/1 East Africa: British Cultural Propaganda—General (1941-46)
BW8/1 Nigeria: British Council House, Lagos (1944-46)
BW8/2 Library Training Scheme (1942-46)
BW8/4 Nigeria: Library Activities and Reports (1946-47)
BW8/5 Nigeria: British Cultural Propaganda (1939-46)
BW8/7 Libraries: Policy (1942-49)
BW104/2 "A Survey to Ascertain the Existing Available Reading Material in the Federation of Malaya and the Present Provision of Books and Other Literature," by K.D. Ferguson, with Related Papers (1950-51)
BW128/2 Library Reports (1948-60) (consulted when still in the Council's Archives, London, as file NIG/260/20)
BW128/3 Library Development (1959-60) (consulted when still in the Council's Archives, as file NIG/265/14)

Carnegie Corporation of New York
  Bishop, Dr. W.W., 1935-1942
  British Honduras Library (The Jubilee Library)
  Kenya Colony—Library Development in
  McMillan Memorial Library
  Nigeria, West Africa, Support of a Program of Library Development in
  West Africa—Library Development 1936-1945

Ford Foundation, New York
  PA61-66 Program Specialists and Consultants on Library Development in
    Nigeria
  PA63-01 Establishment of a National Library in Nigeria

Girton College, Cambridge
  M.C. Bradbrook, "Strong Minded Dons," 1993 typescript
  Papers of Ethel Sophia Fegan

School of Oriental and African Studies, University of London
  Papers of C.G. Richards, PP.MS. 12

University of Illinois at Urbana-Champaign, University Archives
  Ferguson, Kate Dorothy, placement file

Bibliography

Afigbo, A.E. "The Social Repercussions of Colonial Rule: The New Social Structures." In *General History of Africa,* vol. 7, *Africa under Colonial Domination,* ed. A. Adu Boahen, 487-507. Paris: UNESCO, 1985.

[African Publishers Network]. "Approaches to Book Provision in Africa: The APNET Perspective. A Synthesis of Major Issues with Recommendations . . . for Submission to the World Bank in Support of the APNET Visit . . . 8th to 10th December 1993."

Aguolu, C.C. "The Foundations of Modern Libraries in Nigeria." *International Library Review* 9 (1977): 461-83.

Aguolu, C.C. "Libraries as Agents of Research and Scholarship, with Special Reference to Borno State." *Annals of Borno* 1 (1983): 17-28.

Aje, Simeon B. "National Libraries in Developing Countries." In *Advances in Librarianship* no. 12, 105-43. New York: Academic Press, 1977.

Aje, S.B. "Public Libraries in Western Nigeria: A General Survey." *WALA News* 2 (1956): 78-84.

Alemna, A.A. "Scientific and Technical Information in Ghana." *Information Development* 8 (1992): 215-20.

Allen, Joan. "Books Mean Progress: The Public Library & N.A. Reading Rooms in Northern Nigeria." *WALA News* 4 (1961): 4-10.

Allen, Joan. "Early Days in the Northern Regional Library, Kaduna." *Northern Nigeria Library Notes* no. 2 (1964/65): 71-74.

Allen, Joan. "Summary of the Sharr Report 'The Library Needs of Northern Nigeria' with Some Comments." *Northern Nigeria Library Notes* no. 1 (1964): 4-19.

Altbach, Philip G., ed. *Publishing and Development in the Third World.* London: Hans Zell, 1992.

Altbach, Philip G. "What We Know about Third World Publishing." In *Bibliography on Publishing and Book Development in the Third World, 1980-1993,* comp. Philip G. Altbach and Hyaeweol Choi, 1-26. Bellagio Studies in Publishing no. 3. Norwood, N.J.: Ablex Publishing, 1993.

Amadi, Adolphe O. *African Libraries: Western Tradition and Colonial Brainwashing.* Metuchen, N.J.: Scarecrow Press, 1981.

Amin, Samir. *Neo-Colonialism in West Africa.* New York: Monthly Review Press, 1973.

Anderson, Florence. *Carnegie Corporation: Library Program 1911-1961.* New York: Carnegie Corporation of New York, 1963.

Arnove, Robert F., ed. *Philanthropy and Cultural Imperialism: The Foundations at Home and Abroad.* Boston: G.K. Hall, 1980.

Atherton, Lucy. "Community Libraries in Zimbabwe." *Information Development* 9 (1993): 36-43.

Ayandele, E.A. *The Educated Elite in the Nigerian Society.* Ibadan: Ibadan University Press, 1974.

Ballara, Marcela. *Women and Literacy.* London: Zed Books, 1992.

Bayart, Jean-François. *The State in Africa: The Politics of the Belly.* London: Longman, 1993.

Benge, Ronald Charles. *Cultural Crisis and Libraries in the Third World.* London: Clive Bingley, 1979.

Benge, R.C. "Library Objectives in Africa." In *Confessions of a Lapsed Librarian,* 206-20. Metuchen, N.J.: Scarecrow, 1984.

Benge, Ronald. "Return to West Africa: Some Notes on Library Education in Africa." *Nigerian Libraries* 9 (1973): 97-100.

Benge, R.C. "Some Notes on Reading in Ghana." *Library World* 64 (1963): 210-13.

Borland, E.A. "Ten Years of the Carnegie Non-European Library, Transvaal: 1931-1941." *South African Libraries* 10 (1942): 1-6.

Broome, E.M. "Books for the People: An Experiment in Library Service in Tanganyika." In *Library Work in Africa,* ed. Anna-Britta Wallenius, 59-71. Uppsala: Scandinavian Institute of African Studies, 1966.

Burns, [Sir] Alan. *Colonial Civil Servant.* London: Allen & Unwin, 1949.

Canadian Organization for Development through Education. *The Zambia Children's Book Project.* Oxford: CODE—Europe, 1994.

Carnell, Jessie, and John Harris. "Libraries in Nigeria: A Memorandum Presented to the Study Group on Education in West Africa, 1951/52." *West African Libraries* 1 (1954): 2-6.

Carpenter, Julie, and others. "The Book Sector in Zambian Education: A Study Prepared for the Delegate of the Commission of the European Communities and the Government of the Republic of Zambia." 1990.

Chakava, Henry. "Kenyan Publishing: Independence and Dependence." In *Publishing and Development in the Third World,* ed. Philip G. Altbach, 119-50. London: Hans Zell, 1992.

Chakava, Henry. "Private Enterprise Publishing in Kenya: A Long Struggle for Emancipation." *Logos* 4 (1993): 130-35.

Clow, David. "Aid and Development—The Context of Library-Related Aid." *Libri* 36 (1986): 85-97.

Clow, David. "Blood from Stones: A Polemic on the Funding of Library Services in Third World Countries." In *Nothing to Read? The Crisis of Document Provision in the Third World,* ed. D.J. Membrey, 97-107. Edgbaston [Birmingham]: International and Comparative Librarianship Group of the Library Association, 1990.

Cole, Patrick. *Modern and Traditional Elites in the Politics of Lagos.* Cambridge: Cambridge University Press, 1975.

Coombs, Douglas. *Spreading the Word: The Library Work of the British Council.* London: Mansell, 1988.

Davidson, Basil. *The Black Man's Burden: Africa and the Curse of the Nation-State.* London: James Currey, 1992.

Davies, Robert. "Uganda" [Final report of the country focus group in the study conducted under the auspices of the International Library and Information Action for Development—Higher Education Information Development Research Project]. 1993.

Development of Public Libraries in Africa: The Ibadan Seminar. Paris: UNESCO, 1954.

Dillsworth, Gloria E. "The Sierra Leone National Public Library Service." In *Information and Libraries in the Developing World,* vol. 1, *Sub-Saharan Africa,* ed. Michael Wise and Anthony Olden, 107-23. London: Library Association, 1990.

Domont, J.M. "Reading in the Belgian Congo." In *Development of Public Libraries in Africa,* 77-81. Paris: UNESCO, 1954.

Donaldson, Frances. *The British Council: The First Fifty Years.* London: Jonathan Cape, 1984.

Durrani, Shiraz. "Agricultural Informa tion Services in Kenya and Third World Needs." *Journal of Librarianship* 19 (1987): 108-20.

Durrani, Shiraz. "Independence in Kenya and the Lost Opportunity to Build a People Oriented Library Service." *Focus on International and Comparative Librarianship,* forthcoming.

Durrani, Shiraz. "Libraries, Communication and Development in Kenya: The Missing Political Factor." In *Information and Libraries in the Developing World,* vol. 1, *Sub-Saharan Africa,* ed. Michael Wise and Anthony Olden, 159-70. London: Library Association, 1990.

Durrani, Shiraz. "The Mirage of Democracy in Kenya: People's Struggle for Information as an Aspect of the Struggle for Liberation." Paper presented at the Emerging Democracies and Freedom of Information Conference of the International Group of the Library Association, Somerville College, Oxford, 2-4 September 1994.

East Africa High Commission. East African Literature Bureau. *Annual Report,* 1950- . Nairobi: Government Printer.

Evans, Evelyn J.A. *The Development of Public Library Services in the Gold Coast.* London: Library Association, 1956.

Evans, Evelyn J.A. "[Ethel] Fegan" [Obituary]. *Library Association Record* 77 (1975): 299.

Evans, Evelyn J.A. "Library Services in Ghana." In *Library Work in Africa,* ed. Anna-Britta Wallenius, 1-17. Uppsala: Scandinavian Institute of African Studies, 1966.

Evans, Evelyn. "The Public Library and the Community." *WALA News* 3 (1959): 147-56.

Evans, Evelyn J.A. *A Tropical Library Service: The Story of Ghana's Libraries.* London: Andre Deutsch, 1964.

Evenden, Dawn E. "The Johannesburg Public Library: A Personal View of Some of the Events of the Last Fifteen Years." In *A World Too Wide: Essays on Libraries and Other Themes in Honour of Reuben Musiker,* ed. Joseph Sherman, 111-23. Johannesburg: University of the Witwatersrand Library, 1993.

Expert Meeting on National Planning of Documentation and Library Services in Africa: Kampala, Uganda, 7-15 December 1970: Final Report. Paris: UNESCO, 1971.

Fanon, Frantz. *The Wretched of the Earth.* New York: Grove Press, 1968.

Faseyi, J.A.O. "Library Service in the North Central State: The Past, Present and Future." Mimeo, 1976.

Faseyi, J.A. "Public Library Serice in the Former Northern Nigeria." *Nigerian Libraries* 4 (1968): 68-75.

Fegan, E.S. "Life in a Leper Colony in Nigeria." *Girton Review*, Easter Term 1946, 16-19.

Fegan, Ethel S.] "Report on Library Needs in British West Africa." West Africa—Library Development 1936-1945 file, Carnegie Corporation of New York archives.

Fegan, E.S. "Some Africans." *Girton Review*, Michaelmas Term 1929, 10-14.

[Fegan, Ethel S.] "Tour of British West Africa for the Carnegie Corporation, N.Y. 1941-2." Two handwritten notebooks. Girton College archives.

Ferguson, Kate D. "A Survey to Ascertain the Existing Reading Material in the Federation of Malaya and the Present Provision of Books and Other Literature." 1950. BW104/2, Public Record Office, London.

Ferguson, Milton J. *Memorandum: Libraries in the Union of South Africa, Rhodesia, and Kenya Colony.* New York: Carnegie Corporation of New York, 1929.

Flood, R.A. *Public Libraries in the Colonies.* London: Library Association, 1951.

"Footsteps in Librarianship: Miss Priscilla M. Allen Talks to *Maktaba* About Her Past Experiences on the Occasion of Her Final Retirement from Active Library Practice in East Africa, 1 July 1976." *Maktaba* 4 (1977): 28-36.

Fox, James. *White Mischief.* London: Jonathan Cape, 1982.

Frank, Andre Gunder. *Latin America: Underdevelopment or Revolution: Essays on the Development of Underdevelopment and the Immediate Enemy.* New York: Monthly Review Press, 1969.

Friis, Theodorus. *The Public Library in South Africa: An Evaluative Study.* Cape Town: Afrikaanse Pers-Boekhandel, 1962.

Frost, Richard. *Race Against Time: Human Relations and Politics in Kenya Before Independence.* London: Rex Collings, 1978.

Gardner, F.M. "The Final Page." *Library Association Record* 67 (1965): 13-14.

Gardner, F.M. "The President's Page." *Library Association Record* 66 (1964): 585-87.

Ghana: Libraries and Information Profile 1987. London: British Council, 1987.

Goldhor, Herbert. *An Introduction to Scientific Research in Librarianship.* Urbana, Ill.: University of Illinois, Graduate School of Library Science, 1972.

Graham-Brown, Sarah. *Education in the Developing World: Conflict and Crisis.* London: Longman, 1991.

Guthrie, Malcolm. "Report of an Investigation in the British Dependencies of East and Central Africa." [1944]. BW7/1, Public Record Office, London.

Gwandu, Alhaji Umaru. "Presidential Address." *WALA News* 4 (1961): 48-52.

Harris, John. *Ibadan University Library: Some Notes on Its Birth and Growth.* Ibadan: Ibadan University Press, 1968.

Harris, John. "Libraries and Librarianship in Nigeria at Mid-Century." *Nigerian Libraries* 6 (1970): 26-40.

Harris, Michael H. "The Dialectic of Defeat: Antinomies in Research in Library and Information Science." *Library Trends* 34 (1986): 515-31.

Harrity, Sara. "'Extracting the Gold' from Book Surpluses." *Logos* 5 (1994): 153-57.

Hill, Alan. *In Pursuit of Publishing.* London: John Murray, 1988.

Hill, F.W.G. "Strategic Planning for University Libraries: Welcome to Workshop Participants." In *Survival Strategies in African University Libraries,* ed. Helga Atkinson Patrikios and Lisbeth A. Levey, 7-10. Washington, D.C.: AAAS, 1994.

Hockey, S.W. *Development of Library Services in East Africa: A Report Submitted to the Governments of East Africa.* 1960.

Horrocks, S.H. "Eastern Region and UNESCO Public Library Pilot Project." *WALA News* 3 (1958): 12-16.

Houle, Cyril O. *Libraries in Adult and Fundamental Education: The Report of the Malmö Seminar.* Paris: UNESCO, 1951.

Huxley, Elspeth. *Literature for Africans: Report.* 1946.

Huxley, Elspeth. *Out in the Midday Sun: My Kenya.* London: Chatto and Windus, 1985.

Huxley, Elspeth, and Margery Perham. *Race and Politics in Kenya.* London: Faber, 1944.

Ilomo, C.S. "The History and Work of Tanzania Library Service 1963-80." In *Aspects of African Librarianship,* ed. Michael Wise, 98-153. London and New York: Mansell, 1985.

Ishola, Sunday Oladele. "The Development of Public Libraries in Nigeria." Fellowship of the Library Association thesis, London, 1976.

Joll, James. *Antonio Gramsci.* New York: Penguin, 1978.

Kaungamno, E.E., and C.S. Ilomo. *Books Build Nations.* 2 vols. London and Dar es Salaam: Transafrica Book Distributors and Tanzania Library Service, 1979.

Kemp, D.A.R. "A View of Kenya Libraries." *The Librarian and Book World* 48 (1959): 157-62.

Kennedy, R.F. *The Heart of a City: A History of the Johannesburg Public Library.* Cape Town: Juta and Company, 1970.

Kluzek, Irene. "The Library of the Nigerian Institute of International Affairs." *Nigerian Libraries* 4 (1968): 76-78.

Kotei, Samuel Isaac Asharley. "The Social Determinants of Library Development in Ghana with Reference to the Influence of British Traditions." M.Phil thesis, University of London, 1972.

Lagos Library. "Report for . . . 1932"- . Nigeria (West Africa) Support of a Program of Library Development file. Carnegie Corporation of New York archives.

Lancour, Harold. *Libraries in British West Africa: A Report of a Survey for the Carnegie Corporation of New York, October-November 1957.* University of Illinois Library School Occasional Paper no. 53. Urbana: 1958.

Lessing, Doris. *African Laughter: Four Visits to Zimbabwe.* London: Harper Collins, 1992.

Levey, Lisbeth A. *A Profile of Research Libraries in Sub-Saharan Africa: Acquisitions, Outreach, and Infrastructure.* Washington, D.C.: AAAS, Sub-Saharan Africa Program, 1993.

"Libraries and the West African Community: A Talk Given . . . [by K. Middlemast] . . . with Notes on the Discussion." *WALA News* 2 (1955): 27-31.

Lieberman, Irving. *A Survey of the Lagos City Library.* Lagos: Lagos City Council, 1964.

Lungu, C.M.B. "Review of Urban Public Library Educational Services (UPLES) in Kitwe, Zambia: A Survey." In *Proceedings of the Info Africa Nova Conference 1993,* vol. 1, ed. A.G. Coetzer, 231-44. Pretoria: Info Africa Nova, 1993.

Maack, Mary N. "The Colonial Legacy in West African Libraries: A Comparative Analysis." In *Advances in Librarianship* no. 12, 173-245. New York: Academic Press, 1982.

Maack, Mary Niles. *Libraries in Senegal: Continuity and Change in an Emerging Nation.* Chicago: American Library Association, 1981.

Maack, Mary Niles. "The Role of External Aid in West African Library Development." *Library Quarterly* 56 (1986): 1-16.

Macmillan, Mona. *Champion of Africa: The Second Phase of the Work of W.M. Macmillan, 1934-1974.* Long Wittenham, Oxfordshire: Mona Macmillan, 1985.

Made, S.M., and G.C. Motsi. "Alternative Ways of Providing Rural Information. Culture Houses: The Zimbabwean Experience." *Zimbabwe Librarian* 18 (1986): 4-6.

Maloba, Wunyabari. "Nationalism and Decolonization, 1947-1963." In *A Modern History of Kenya 1895-1980: in Honour of B.A. Ogot,* ed. William R. Ochieng', 173-201. Nairobi: Evans Brothers [Kenya], 1989.

McGregor, Charles. "Raiding the World Bank." *Bookseller* (15 July 1994), 32-33.

Mchombu, K.J. "African Information Services: The Search for a Role. A Keynote Address." In *Proceedings of the Info Africa Nova Conference 1993,* vol. 1, ed. A.G. Coetzer, 1-16. Pretoria: Info Africa Nova, 1993.

Mchombu, K.J. "Alternatives to the National Library in Less Developed Countries." *Libri* 35 (1985): 227-49.

Mchombu, K.J. "Development of Library and Documentation Services in Tanzania: Problems of Strategy and Tactics." *Information Processing and Management* 20 (1984): 559-69.

Mchombu, K.J., and K. Miti. "Formulation of National Information Policies in Africa: Some Unlearnt Lessons." *International Information and Library Review* 24 (1992): 139-71.

Mchombu, Kingo J. "Information Needs for Rural Development: The Case Study of Malawi." *African Journal of Library, Archives and Information Science* 2 (1992): 17-32.

Mchombu, K.J. "On the Librarianship of Poverty." *Libri* 32 (1982): 241-50.

Mchombu, Kingo. "Which Way African Librarianship?" *IFLA Journal* 17 (1991): 26-38.

McMillan Memorial Library and East African (Carnegie) Circulating Libraries. *Annual Report of the Librarian for the Year Ended December 31st, 1953.*

Menou, Michel J., ed. *Measuring the Impact of Information on Development.* Ottawa: International Development Research Centre, 1993.

Moys, Elizabeth M., and C.C. Momoh, eds. *Directory of Lagos Libraries.* Lagos: Oceana Publications, 1965.

National Library of Nigeria. *Annual Report, 1967/68.* Lagos: National Library of Nigeria, 1969.

Ndegwa, John. *Printing and Publishing in Kenya: An Outline of Development.* London: Standing Conference on Library Materials on Africa, 1973.

"A New Lagos Library." *West Africa* (29 October 1932), 1118.

Newa, John M. "The Sustainability of Information Technology Innovations: CD-ROM at the University of Dar es Salaam." In *Survival Strategies in African University Libraries,* ed. Helga Atkinson Patrikios and Lisbeth A. Levey, 77-83. Washington, D.C.: AAAS, 1994.

Ng'ang'a, James M. "Reading at Home and How to Develop Home Libraries." In *Children's Reading Needs: The Challenges of the Next Century to Parents, Educators, Publishers and Librarians in Africa,* ed. Serah W. Mwanycky, 22-26. Nairobi: CHISCI Press, 1993.

Ngwira, Margaret. "Information Delivery in Malawi with Special Emphasis on the Bunda College of Agriculture Library." In *Survival Strategies in African University Libraries*, ed. Helga Atkinson Patrikios and Lisbeth A. Levey, 85-91. Washington, D.C.: AAAS, 1994.

"Nigeria Letter: The Tom Jones Memorial at Lagos." *West Africa* (20 June 1931), 747.

Nigeria, Northern. *Annual Report of the Regional Library Service for 1957.* Kaduna: no date.

Nigeria, Northern. *Annual Report of the Regional Library Service for 1958.* Kaduna: Ministry of Education, Regional Library Division, no date.

Nigeria, Northern. Ministry of Education. *Annual Report of the Regional Library Division 1959.* Kaduna: Government Printer, no date.

Nigeria, Northern. Ministry of Information. *Annual Report of the Regional Library Division, Ministry of Information 1961-1963.* Kaduna: Government Printer, 1964.

Nigeria, Northern. Ministry of Information. *The Library Needs of Northern Nigeria: A Report Prepared Under the Special Commonwealth African Assistance Plan* [by F.A. Sharr]. Kaduna: Government Printer, 1963.

Nigeria, Northern. *Progress and Preparation: A Report on the Activities of the Library Division Ministry of Information Northern Nigeria 1st April, 1963-31st March, 1966.* Kaduna: Government Printer, 1966.

Niven, [Sir] Rex. *Nigerian Kaleidoscope: Memoirs of a Colonial Servant.* London: C. Hurst, 1982.

Nuhu, Ahmed. "Public Librarianship in Northern Nigeria: Limitations and Challenges." *African Journal of Library, Archives and Information Science* 4 (1994): 27-36.

Nwankwo, Victor U. "Publishing in Nigeria Today." In *Publishing and Development in the Third World*, ed. Philip G. Altbach, 151-68. London: Hans Zell, 1992.

Nwikina, Gbole N. "On the Lighter Side: Random Jottings." *Nigerian Libraries* 1 (1964): 142-47.

Nwikina, Gbole N. "Reading Habits of Nigerians." In *Development of Public Libraries in Africa: The UNESCO Seminar*, 68-76. Paris: UNESCO, 1954.

O'Connor, Brigid, and Stephan Roman. "Building Bridges with Books: The British Council's Sixty-Year Record." *Logos* 5 (1994): 133-38.

Oddoye, D.E.M. "Ghana Library Board." In *Aspects of African Librarianship*, ed. Michael Wise, 69-97. London and New York: Mansell, 1985.

Odumosu, Olu. "Reflections on the Beginnings." *Nigerbiblios* 9 (1984): 137-39.

Oduyoye, Modupe. "The Role of Christian Publishing Houses in Africa Today." In *Publishing in Africa in the Seventies,* ed. Edwina Oluwasanmi, Eva McLean and Hans Zell, 209-32. Ile-Ife: University of Ife Press, 1975.

Ojiambo, Joseph B. "Kenya, Library and Information Services in." In *Encyclopedia of Library and Information Science,* 45 (suppl. 10): 198-221. New York: Marcel Dekker, 1990.

Okorie, Kalu. "Lagos Municipal Library: A Brief Introduction." *West African Libraries* 1 (1954): 7-8.

Okorie, Kalu. "Public Libraries." *WALA News* 3 (1960): 231-37.

Olden, Anthony. "Alan Burns, the Lagos Library, and the Commencement of Carnegie Support for Library Development in British West Africa." *Journal of Library History* 22 (1987): 397-408.

Olden, Anthony. "Constraints on the Development of Public Library Service in Nigeria." *Library Quarterly* 55 (1985): 398-423.

Olden, Anthony. "Sub-Saharan Africa and the Paperless Society." *Journal of the American Society for Information Science* 38 (1987): 298-304.

Omolewa, Michael. "Adult Readers in Nigerian Libraries, 1932-1960: A Study of Library Use in Colonial Nigeria." *Nigerian Libraries* 10 (1974): 29-40.

Opondo, R.G. "Nairobi City Council Libraries." *Maktaba* 1 (1974): 65-74.

Panofsky, Hans E. "National Libraries and Bibliographies in Africa." In *Comparative and International Librarianship,* ed. Miles M. Jackson, Jr., 229-55. Westport, Conn.: Greenwood Publishing Corporation, 1970.

Parkes, Joan. "The Regional Library Service in Northern Nigeria." *West African Libraries* 1 (1954): 7-9.

Patrikios, Helga Atkinson. "A Minimal Acquisitions Policy for Journals at the University of Zimbabwe Medical Library." In *Survival Strategies,* ed. Helga Atkinson Patrikios and Lisbeth A. Levey, 93-99. Washington, D.C.: AAAS, 1994.

Patrikios, Helga Atkinson, and Lisbeth A. Levey, eds. *Survival Strategies in African University Libraries: New Technologies in the Service of Information.* Washington, D.C.: AAAS, 1994.

Pattison, Bruce. *Special Relations: The University of London and New Universities Overseas, 1947-1970.* London: University of London, 1984.

Pearce, Robert. "Library Services in the New States of Nigeria: A Report Prepared for the Ministry of Information, Federal Government of Nigeria, under the Special Commonwealth African Assistance Plan." 1968. NIG/265/14, Archives Section, British Council, London.

Perham, Margery. *Colonial Sequence: 1930 to 1949: A Chronological Commentary upon British Colonial Policy Especially in Africa.* London: Methuen, 1967.

[Perham, Margery]. "Cultural Relations Between Britain and the African Dependencies." BW2/93. Public Record Office, London.

Perham, Margery. *West African Passage: A Journey through Nigeria, Chad and the Cameroons, 1931-1932*, ed. A.H.M. Kirk-Greene. London: Peter Owen, 1983.

Piggott, Mary. "Edith Jessie Carnell" [Obituary]. *Library Association Record* 86 (1984): 319.

Pitt, S.A. *Memorandum: Libraries in the Union of South Africa, Rhodesia, and Kenya Colony.* New York: Carnegie Corporation of New York, 1929.

Priestley, Carol. *The Commonwealth Higher Education Support Scheme: Study on a Commonwealth Journal Distribution Programme. Final Report.* [London]: Commonwealth Secretariat, 1992.

Priestley, Carol. "The Difficult Art of Book Aid: An African Survey." *Logos* 4 (1993): 215-21.

Priestley, Carol. "Higher Education Learning Resource Materials: The State of Play of Libraries and Books Development." *Science, Technology and Development* 9 (1991): 18-34.

Priestley, Carol. *SAREC Library Support Programme Evaluation and Review: Ethiopia, Mozambique and Tanzania.* Stockholm: Swedish Agency for Research Cooperation with Developing Countries, 1993.

"Priscilla Harris: Obituary." *New Zealand Libraries* 37 (1974): 136-37.

Proceedings of the Conference on Textbook Provision and Library Development in Africa, Manchester, October 1991. Manchester: British Council, 1992.

"Public Library Manifesto." *UNESCO Bulletin for Libraries* 3 (1949): 242-44.

Ransom, David. "Ford Country: Building an Elite for Indonesia." In *The Trojan Horse: A Radical Look at Foreign Aid*, ed. Steve Weissman and others, 93-116. San Francisco: Ramparts Press, 1974.

Rappaport, Philip. "Libraries and Library Development in Nigeria: An Assessment of Present Trends and Recommendations for Future Government Involvement and Policy." 1971. Ford Foundation Archives, Report 004235.

Rappaport, Philip. "Libraries in Nigeria: Background Paper on the Development of Libraries in Nigeria Presented . . . to Ford Foundation Seminar, March 15-17, 1971." Ford Foundation Archives, Report 004234.

Raseroka, H.K. "Changes in Public Libraries During the Last Twenty Years: An African Perspective." *Libri* 44 (1994): 153-63.

Report of Mr. Milton J. Ferguson on the Libraries in the Union of South Africa, Rhodesia, and Kenya Colony. New York: Carnegie Corporation of New York, 1929.

Richards, Charles. "Interview." *African Book Publishing Record* 2 (1976): 161-64.

Richards, Charles Granston. "No Carpet on the Floor: Recollections and Reflections on the Work of 40 Years, 1935 to 1975, in the Development of Literature and Publishing, Chiefly in the Third World." Typescript, Rhodes House, Oxford, and School of Oriental and African Studies, London.

Richards, C.G. "The Work of a Literature Bureau." In *Development of Public Libraries in Africa*, 88-91. Paris: UNESCO, 1954.

Roberts, Andrew. "The Imperial Mind." In *Cambridge History of Africa*, vol. 7, *From 1905 to 1940*, ed. A.D. Roberts, 24-76. Cambridge: Cambridge University Press, 1986.

Rogers, Frank B. "Report of a Survey of Lagos Area Libraries of the Federal Government of Nigeria, 16 February-9 March 1961, for the Ford Foundation." Ford Foundation Archives, PA61-66 attachment file.

Rosenberg, Diana Bryant. "The Colonial State and the Development of Public Libraries in Kenya prior to 1965." Fellowship of the Library Association thesis, London, 1984.

Rosenberg, Diana. "Imposing Libraries: The Establishment of National Public Library Services in Africa, with Particular Reference to Kenya." *Third World Libraries* 4 (1993): 35-44.

Rosenberg, Diana. "Resource Sharing—Is It the Answer for Africa?" *African Journal of Library, Archives and Information Science* 3 (1993): 107-12.

Rosenberg, Diana. "Rural Community Resource Centres: A Sustainable Option for Africa?" *Information Development* 9 (1993): 29-35.

Ryle, John. "The Lost Library of Zanzibar." *Times Literary Supplement* (13 September 1985), 1002.

Sharr, F.A. "The Development of a New Library Service." *Nigerian Libraries* 1 (1964): 8-15.

"Sir Alan Burns: A Tribute." *West Africa* (20 October 1980), 2065-67.

Sitzman, Glenn L. *African Libraries*. Metuchen, N.J.: Scarecrow Press, 1988.

Sjostrom, Margareta, and Rolf Sjostrom. *How Do You Spell Development? A Study of a Literacy Campaign in Ethiopia*. Uppsala: Scandinavian Institute of African Studies, 1983.

Stifel, Laurence D., Davidson, Ralph K., and James S. Coleman, eds. *Social Sciences and Public Policy in the Developing World*. Lexington, Mass.: Lexington Books, 1982.

Sturges, Paul, and Richard Neill. *The Quiet Struggle: Libraries and Information for Africa*. London: Mansell, 1990.

Sutton, Francis X. "Foundations and Cultural Development of the Third World." In *Philanthropy and Culture: The International Foundation Perspective,* ed. Kathleen D. McCarthy, 137-55. Philadelphia: University of Philadelphia Press for the Rockefeller Foundation, 1984.

Taylor, William. "A Review of ODA Support to the Ranfurly Library Service (Book Aid International)." 1994. Book Aid International archives.

Uba, D.E. "Libraries in the African Development Projects: The Problems of the Library Service in Africa." In *Libraries and National Development (Final Report of the Third Afro-Nordic Library Conference, Finland, 3-7 September, 1979),* 177-92. [Paris]: UNESCO, no date.

[Vischer, Sir Hanns, and Margaret Wrong]. "Libraries: Nigeria, Gold Coast, Sierra Leone, and Gambia." [1939]. West Africa—Library Development 1936-1945 file, Carnegie Corporation of New York archives.

Wall, Joseph Frazier. *Andrew Carnegie.* New York: Oxford University Press, 1970.

Wallenius, Anna-Britta, ed. *Libraries in East Africa.* Uppsala: Scandinavian Institute of African Studies, 1971.

Wallenius, Anna-Britta, ed. *Library Work in Africa.* Uppsala: Scandinavian Institute of African Studies, 1966.

White, Carl M. *The National Library of Nigeria: Growth of the Idea, Problems and Progress.* Lagos: Federal Ministry of Information, 1964.

Wise, Michael, ed. *Aspects of African Librarianship: A Collection of Writings.* London: Mansell, 1985.

Wise, Michael, and Anthony Olden, eds. *Information and Libraries in the Developing World,* vol. 1, *Sub-Saharan Africa.* London: Library Association, 1990.

Wise, Michael, ed. *Survival Under Adverse Conditions: Proceedings of the African Library Science Journals Workshop.* The Hague: International Federation of Library Associations and Institutions, 1994.

Index

About the Author

Anthony Olden (B.A., National University of Ireland; Dip. Lib. Inf. Stud., The Queen's University of Belfast; M.L.S., Ahmadu Bello University, Nigeria; Ph.D., University of Illinois; A.L.A.), is a Senior Lecturer at Thames Valley University, London. He has worked in public libraries in Ireland, and in university libraries and teaching in Nigeria and the U.S. He has also taught short courses in China and Kenya. Dr. Olden has contributed articles to academic and professional journals, and is joint editor of the Information and Libraries in the Developing World series (The Library Association, London).

SOCIAL SCIENCE LIBRARY

Oxford University Library Services
Manor Road
Oxford OX1 3UQ
Tel: (2)71093 (enquiries and renewals)
http://www.ssl.ox.ac.uk

This is a NORMAL LOAN item.

We will email you a reminder before this item is due.

Please see http://www.ssl.ox.ac.uk/lending.html
for details on:

- loan policies; these are also displayed on the notice boards and in our library guide.

- how to check when your books are due back.

- how to renew your books, including information on the maximum number of renewals. Items may be renewed if not reserved by another reader. Items must be renewed before the library closes on the due date.

- level of fines; fines are charged on overdue books.

Please note that this item may be recalled during Term.